Migration

Made in India by Satinder Chohan, Tamasha national tour 2017

'Tamasha is a mirror reflecting a nation of continuing change and creativity, of mixings and mergings. British culture needs reminding it has always been global. Tamasha's stirring, audacious work makes sure the nation never forgets what it is.'

Yasmin Alibhai-Brown, cultural commentator

Tamasha: Contemporary British theatre at its best

Tamasha is Britain's leading touring theatre company producing new plays inspired by the diversity of our globalised world. Our work places the voices of emerging and established artists from culturally diverse backgrounds centre-stage. Landmark productions include *East Is East* (1996), *Balti Kings* (2001), *A Fine Balance* (2006), *Snookered* (2012), *My Name Is . . .* (2014), *Made in India* (2017) and *Approaching Empty* (2019). We have a proud history of changing lives, propelling unknown talent into tomorrow's leading artists, launching the careers of many household names including Parminder Nagra (*Bend It Like Beckham*), Jimi Mistry (*East Is East*) and Raza Jaffrey (*Homeland*). We continue to nurture the next generation through our Tamasha Developing Artists programme, which is free to join: http://www.tamasha.org.uk/developing-artists/about-tda

Education projects

Tamasha's artistic director, playwright Fin Kennedy, has a 15-year history working with inner-city schools, co-creating plays with students and training teachers in using playwriting techniques in the classroom. For Tamasha, Fin pioneered *Schoolwrights*, the UK's first coordinated playwrights-in-schools training programme, and founded Tamasha Playwrights, an in-house group trained to work as writers-in-residence in urban schools. This group of 43 (and growing) diverse emerging professional playwrights is now available to hire – anything from a one-off workshop to a bespoke new play for young people. Tamasha Playwrights are also trained as producers and fundraisers, to work with schools to help raise the money together for more ambitious projects.

For more information, including a quote, or to discuss working with Tamasha to fundraise for a project in your school: admin@tamasha.org.uk / 020 7749 0090 / www.tamasha.org.uk

Migration Plays

Four Large Cast Ensemble Stories for Teenagers

Edited by

FIN KENNEDY

methuen | drama

LONDON • NEW YORK • OXFORD • NEW DELHI • SYDNEY

METHUEN DRAMA
Bloomsbury Publishing Plc
50 Bedford Square, London, WC1B 3DP, UK
1385 Broadway, New York, NY 10018, USA

BLOOMSBURY, METHUEN DRAMA and the Methuen Drama logo are trademarks
of Bloomsbury Publishing Plc

First published in Great Britain 2019

Cover design by Louise Dugdale
Cover image © Daily Herald Archive / The National Science and Media Museum /
Science & Society Picture Library

A catalogue record for this book is available from the British Library.

A catalog record for this book is available from the Library of Congress.

ISBN: PB: 978-1-3500-9041-5
       ePDF: 978-1-3500-9042-2
       eBook: 978-1-3500-9044-6

Typeset by RefineCatch Limited, Bungay, Suffolk
Printed and bound in India

Contents

Introduction

Migration Stories was a Tamasha schools project delivered by playwrights and directors working in several different secondary schools in London and Derby. The format involved twenty-five Drama students from Years 7 to 10 coming off-timetable for a day and participating in exercises designed to unpack their thoughts and feelings on the topic of migration, and encourage them to respond creatively to what they were learning. These sessions were facilitated by the director, with the playwright taking notes. Each playwright then went away and worked up the ideas generated into a twenty-minute script for performance, with parts for the whole class.

In a second full-day workshop each writer presented the script back to their group and the students worked towards rehearsing it with the director for a script-in-hand performance after school to an invited audience of friends, families and teachers. Each script was then left with each Drama teacher to continue to rehearse it into a more polished performance, or for use again with a new group.

We are delighted to be able to share both some of our exercises and the play texts they generated in this unique anthology. Migration as a subject seems more pressing and relevant in twenty-first-century Britain with each passing day. It is critical that we are able to have an informed debate about it, particularly with young people. We firmly believe, and this project shows, that participatory theatre projects are uniquely placed to do this – and can involve the heart as well as the head. We hope that the material contained in this volume will empower teachers and young people around the country to create their own plays, and have their own debates with sensitivity, intelligence and empathy.

Fin Kennedy
Artistic Director, Tamasha
www.tamasha.org.uk

Foreword

We are creating a Migration Museum for Britain – a moving and inspiring institution that puts Britain's important migration story at the forefront of our national consciousness. Migration is a pressing contemporary issue and it lies at the centre of debates about Britishness and belonging, identity and inclusion. Migration is much more than an issue to be addressed or a problem to be solved – it's a human story that connects us all going back thousands of years. If you peel back the layers of anybody's family history in Britain, you find a migration story – whether immigration, emigration, or both. There is no simple narrative, and certainly there are no simplistic conclusions to be drawn. But if we understood Britain's migration history better, we would have a better understanding of who we are today, as individuals and as a nation.

Since 2013 we have staged a range of exhibitions and events, and developed a far-reaching education programme. Young people have been at the heart of who we are and what we are trying to achieve from the outset. We have now engaged directly with over 7,000 young people from primary schools, secondary schools and universities from across the UK as well as visiting international groups.

Key to our education programme has been testing out different approaches to migration learning, based on themes explored in our varied exhibitions. It is in that spirit that we embarked on the *Migration Stories* theatre-in-education project with Tamasha. It was exciting to see how Tamasha took our initial ideas and worked them into something involving deep connections between a raft of amazing playwrights and directors and our participating schools in London and Derby. Each of these theatre professionals brought something different to the project, and shared their own migration stories with the pupils. It was our first exploration of using drama as a tool for migration learning. We had an independent research group evaluate the project, and they found that drama was an effective vehicle for exploring and challenging attitudes to immigration. Feedback from participating pupils attested to the fact that drama allows for empathy in ways that are more limited in 'normal' classroom settings. This project very much chimes with our collaborative, participatory storytelling ethos, which continues to underpin everything that we do as we develop and grow.

My key highlight throughout this project was witnessing pupils' pride at their thoughts and words being featured in the plays created for them by a professional playwright. Deeper focus groups with participating pupils gave me the opportunity to hear how pupils were engaging at a profound level, beyond what could be seen during script reading and rehearsals.

We are so pleased to be able to share the learning and the scripts as a legacy of this unique project. We believe this approach has enormous potential to deepen migration learning in schools across the UK, and we wish all those embarking on this journey the very best with their endeavours.

Emily Miller
Head of Learning and Partnerships, Migration Museum
www.migrationmuseum.org

Nothing to Declare

Sharmila Chauhan

Author's Note

This play was written as a response to increasing levels of racial intolerance and Brexit. It explores themes around heritage, memories and continuity of culture as part of the process in creating diasporic and new cultures.

As somebody from a 'twice-migrant' family, the idea of keepsakes resonated deeply with me. As a child I remember being very struck by the juxtaposition of wooden elephants, Indian jewellery and Kenyan wall carvings that filled our East London home. There are so many stories and beauty in each one. They reminded me that I was all those things and more. Without these physical reminders, these anchors, many memories, the plurality of identity, are easily lost.

With this in mind I wondered what compromises are being made by people like me on a daily basis. The public resurgence of gross intolerance and bigotry brings to the fore again the question of what people are being asked to give up in order to 'fit into' contemporary Western life.

Nothing to Declare questions notions of integration and assimilation, on a deep and personal level. It asks what we lose when we forget who we are and what a nation loses when it is too afraid to welcome others in.

Characters

Head Immigration Officer, *can be male or female*

Immigration Officers, *played by a group of actors, assist the Head Immigration Officer*

Maya, *British-Indian girl, early twenties*

Joseph, *British-Caribbean boy, early twenties*

Crowd, *played by a group of actors, represent the 'common people' or general population – they speak as a chorus*

Bangles, *can be played by a group of actors*

Dog Tags, *can be played by a group of actors*

Hansa, *Indian woman, early fifties, smart and comes across strict*

Surya, *Hansa's daughter, nineteen – non-speaking part*

Adhiti, *Surya's daughter – non-speaking part*

Sinaed, *Irish woman, early twenties first-generation immigrant, a young romantic*

Skye, *teenager, represents the land*

Aru, *Sinaed's daughter – non-speaking part*

Edward, *Caribbean boy/young man*

William, *Caribbean boy/man*

George, *Caribbean boy/man*

Officer, *army officer – one-line part*

Michael, *Caribbean man, twenty-five – non-speaking part*

River, *teenager, represents the land*

Ann, *Michael's wife, Jamaican woman, twenty-two – one-line part*

Notes

This play takes place in an Arrivals Area/Immigration Centre at an airport or roadside border of an unnamed Western country.

There should be a table with officials behind it. This should be preferably on a raised platform.

There are two signs behind the desk: 'Welcome to Our Country – Please Enter' and 'Entry Denied – Detain or Deport'.

Some of the action also takes place in India, Uganda and the Caribbean (Jamaica – but any English-speaking island would work well).

The piece can be interpreted literally or in a more abstract, surreal way.

There are two keepsake objects: these can be played by several actors as a chorus and can be represented literally by physical objects, costume or just a sign.

– at the start of a line denotes speech that can be spoken by any member of the cast.

/ denotes a character interrupting another character.

Scene One: Welcome . . .

Arrivals Lounge.

Chatter, bustle.

Crowd, *laden with bags and cases, wait in a queue.*

Hidden between them are **Maya** *and* **Bangles**, **Joseph** *and* **Dog Tags**.
Maya *and* **Joseph** *are together.*

Crowd *try to advance towards the 'Welcome to Our Country' sign – an
alarm goes off making the* **Crowd** *retract: confusion, irritation.*

Silence . . .

Immigration Officials *enter. They all wear white and can also wear
white masks.*

Head Immigration Officer   Nothing to declare? Nothing to
declare?!

Waits, uses his baton to point to individuals in the **Crowd** *who look
suspicious.*

Bags are searched. Nothing is found.

Two teenagers, **Skye** *and* **River**, *are part of the* **Crowd** *but don't agree
with it. They might sit apart from everyone else.*

Head Immigration Officer   You! You!

We see the couple **Maya** *and* **Joseph**; *they look different from everyone
else.*

They are brought to the centre of the stage.

Crowd *begin to form groups around each one: at first curious, then they
point and slowly they become afraid, uncomfortable with each one.
Shouting anger and fear.*

Crowd
– Who's that, then?
– Not mine, not ours.
– Foreign, exotic, 'ethnic'.
– Not mine, not ours.
– Don't be-long, don't be here . . .
– Who's that, then?
– Not mine, not ours.

– Foreign, exotic, 'ethnic'.
– Not mine, not ours.
– Don't be-long, don't be here . . .

Head Immigration Officer   ENOUGH!

Silence.

Stand back.

Immigration Officers *walk into the main space. Each carries a long piece of white chalk in their hand.*

During this next section: **Immigration Officers** *use the chalk to draw a line across the stage separating* **Maya** *and* **Joseph** *from everyone else.*

Head Immigration Officer   I see we need a line.

Skye   But why? Lines do not belong here.

Immigration Officers
– Everything needs a line
– A boundary, a place to belong to
– Otherwise you'll be lost.

Head Immigration Officer   Everything over the line is ours . . .
Anything behind it – doesn't belong.

River   So it traps you in . . .?

Head Immigration Officer   No – it keeps the danger out.

Skye   But what happens to everything left out there?

Head Immigration Officer   It stays out. Out of the way. (*Clearing throat.*)
Now state your cases . . .
Who are you and where do you come from?

Maya   Maya – means illusion . . .
Maybe the biggest is 'home'
An illusion, there is no one place
That can be home.

India, Uganda and now England
Travelling through the globe
Our family has travelled thousands of miles
Changed homes, exchanged languages
Given up customs and created new ones

Creating opportunities where there were none
We have never forgotten who we are
Where we have come from . . .

Head Immigration Officer   Holding on to the past is no way of the future!
This could be your home. If you could just let go . . . Next!

Joseph *steps forward.*

Joseph   Joseph – biblical – meaning 'he will add'. We come from a line
of fighters, activists and believers. We are all travellers, aren't we?
Coming from one place and going to another. It is human nature. We take
and give, like a mathematical sum. Whatever the components are, the
result is the same – a human being. I don't mind shifting and changing
because I know who I am . . .

Head Immigration Officer   Clarity! I like that!

Immigration Officers
– The line's been drawn.
– Anything this side is
– 'Our' space.
– Our rules, our customs, our way of life.
– Cross the line and be part of us
– Or stay where they are
– Trapped
– In a place called past . . .

Crowd   Send them back!

Head Immigration Officer   Now, now. Give them a chance!

Some good candidates, with good skills.
Useful skills here in these new citizens.
We may be cautious but we're not stupid!

You will need to make a choice. You can cross the line and start a new life
with us. 'Free' education, 'health care' in one of the greatest democracies
of the world where a 52 per cent majority can change anything!

Doesn't that sound *amazing*?

Maya *and* **Joseph** *nod enthusiastically.*

Head Immigration Officer   You don't need to bring anything here:
values, customs, even language. Everything you need will be provided
for you.

Maya *and* **Joseph** *look a bit worried.*

Head Immigration Officer   So come along! Open to all – but first you must declare.

Maya   Declare?

Immigration Officers   You must declare if you are bringing in any of the following:

- Over-spiced food items, items that reveal religious identity, music that obscures local talent.
- Anything over your Cultural Allowance; for instance, more than two languages or numerous religious holidays.
- Banned or restricted viewpoints in the UK; for example, that racism exists, or that the Empire wasn't great and so on.

Maya   We have nothing to declare.

Joseph   Nothing at all.

Head Immigration Officer *inspects them with suspicion.*

The **Immigration Officers** *come down to inspect their belongings.*

Immigration Officers   Nothing to declare?

Joseph   Not a thing.

Immigration Officers   Nothing to declare . . .?

Maya. Nothing.

They find something.

Immigration Officers   What is this?

Maya   Nothing . . .

Immigration Officers   It looks like some – thing.

Maya   It's nothing.

Immigration Officers   Bangles . . . Dog tags!

They want to take the keepsakes away.

Maya   No! It's nothing.

Joseph   Stop! Wait!

Maya *and* **Joseph** *stop them.*

Immigration Officers   Explain –

Maya   We didn't mean to.

Joseph   We didn't know that, these were restricted.

Maya   They're just ornaments. They have no value

Head Immigration Officer   Ah, but they do, don't they? Otherwise you wouldn't be holding them so tight! Now tell me what they are!

Bangles
– A set of twelve gold bangles.
– Bought in India,
– brought to Uganda, then smuggled to England – We belong to Maya.

Crowd   Go back! Go back! Go back!

Dog Tags
– Military identification
– Numbers are everything
– Who you are – Where you have come from – Where you will go . . .

Crowd (*sung quietly, rising*)
– Shed or leave
– Integrate don't deviate . . .

Head Immigration Officer   You must leave your keepsakes behind!

Maya   But, why?

Crowd (*sung quietly, rising*)
– Shed or leave
– Integrate don't deviate . . .

Skye   Can't they bring something in?
What harm will it do?

Crowd (*escalating*)
– Let some in
– Let them all in . . .
– Let some in
– Let them all in
– Let some in
– Let them all in . . .

River   This is crazy! Surely we should – this is a violation of human rights!

Head Immigration Officer   Now, now . . . Don't be hasty!

Beat.

We're careful, not intolerant.

In the spirit of democracy that this Great Country is built on.

I will give you a chance to rethink your options . . .

Consider what is best for your future . . .

You must decide whether to leave your keepsake or take it along risking deportation . . .

Crowd
– Shed or leave
– Integrate don't deviate . . .
– Be part of us.
– Not a-part from us!

Scene Two: Bangles

Set across three time periods: 1950s India – **Bangles***; early 1971 –* **Sinaed** *and* **Hansa***; and 2016 –* **Maya***.*

Gujarat, India, 1962.

Bangles
– Hidden in the Indian earth
– Dug out by entrepreneurs
– Uncovered by the hand of an old man
– Who used his naked hands to mix in acid
– Who used bare skin to heat it on hot coals
– To extract and purify the gold
– Who sold the precious metal
– At a good price
– To a jeweller
– Who hammered out soft metal into shinning golden disks:
– Who made twelve gold bangles
– Twelve identical gold bangles
– With a deep yellow hue
– As if the Indian sun itself had been melted into us

– Bought secretly by Hansa
– A newly wed with her first child in her stomach
– Before her voyage across the kali pani* to meet her husband in East Africa

---

* 'dark water' (Gujurati)

– She would be prepared for whatever her new life held for her.
– Carefully packed into a red velvet box that kept us protected and
– Hidden, until we arrived in Kampala, Uganda . . .
– Hansa's new life begins . . .

– She hopes it will be a boy . . .
– Her husband works on the Ugandan railways under the British.
– He wants to start his own business.
– Hansa doesn't know whether to believe him or not.
– She barely knows the man she has married.
– Will he be true to his word?
– Or will he deceive her and her dreams?
– She hides us
– All twelve of us
– Knowing that one day they may need them.
– But her husband is true to his word and they set up a business
– They work hard and save money.
– The baby is a girl, they name her Surya after the sun
– The Indian sun, melted into gold – then there's another . . .
– A boy this time, called Chandu
– Gentle like the moon
– Hansa manages the business, her husband has no head for numbers.
– He prefers to sew and make the garments they sell.
– She – Hansa – manages the money.
– She manages it well
– The children and the house too.
– She wears four bangles
– On her right wrist.
– They gently twinkle as she moves
– Twinkle twinkle as she does her daughter's hair
– Twinkle twinkle as she washes the dishes.
– Twinkle twinkle as she laughs and her hands shake.
– Twinkle twinkle as she rubs her husband's head with oil.
– Hansa wants to send Surya to England to be educated.

Hansa *hands* **Surya** *the* **Bangles**.

Bangles
– Everyone says no – even Surya
– But Hansa insists and packs her off, before anyone can object
– She gives her four bangles
– Tells her to keep them safe because – gold is insurance for every
    woman . . .
– Now there are only eight of us left

– Hansa's son Chandu goes off to university in England.
– Apple of her eye
– She mourns his absence
– But Hansa is proud and pleased

– Until he comes home – with a bride
– Sinaed – Irish – green eyes and skin that has never seen the sun.
– Not the African sun . . . nor the yellow Indian sun that shines from her wrists
– Twinkling as she does her hair
– Twinkling as she washes the dishes.
– Twinkling as she laughs and her hands shake.
– Twinkling as she rubs her husband's feet with oil.
– But Hansa is heartbroken

Beat.

Uganda, 1971.

Hansa *and* **Sinaed** *cooking dinner.*

Sinaed   He never said he would be so late.

Hansa   Always add one hour at least to the time he tells you. You'll learn soon enough.

Sinaed   Back home – in London – he was always on time.

Hansa   At 'home' he is not himself. At his home, his mother's home – he can be who he always was. Himself.

Sinaed   And with me?

Hansa   Chandu likes his food spicy.
Let me do it.

Hansa *seasons a pot.*

Sinaed   Can you show me?
So I can make it for him?
Just the way you do.

Beat.

Then **Hansa** *shows her what to do.*

She watches the young bride with a little more approval.

Hansa   That's good. You'll soon learn how to do it.

Sinaed *smiles shyly.*

Hansa   Now finish off making those chapatis.

Bangles
– Love that is young – fresh and courageous.
– Reckless even.
– Is worth its weight.

Beat.

– Always: worth the wait.

Beat.

– Sinaed likes the dance of gold on her mother-in-law's skin.
– She likes the way the sun shines and makes the gold splatter across her
    arms . . .
– But she never says anything
– Time passes, Sinaed is slowly accepted as part of the family.
– Hansa's daughter Surya marries
– Hansa gives Surya two of us when her first grandchild
– Adhiti is born

Hansa *gives* **Adhiti** *two* **Bangles**.

Bangles
– Now there are only six left in the box
– There is wealth and happiness abounds . . .
– Sinaed waits for Hansa to one day love her like a daughter
– But troubled times are ahead.
– In 1973, the president of the country
– Idi Amin orders that the Asian families are to be expelled from Uganda
– Within ninety days taking only fifty-five pounds of cash with them.
– Hansa and Sinaed pack what they can
– How can they pack a whole life into one case?
– How can they say goodbye to the best home they know?

Hansa   Are you ready?

Sinaed   Yes, Ma – I've just done the last case.

Bangles
– She packs the gold inside clothes.
– She packs it inside her shoes and books.
– At last there is nowhere else to hide any more.
– Sinaed takes her Bible and cuts out the pages from inside it.

Sinaed   Here, you can hide your bangles in here.

Hansa *hides the six* **Bangles** *in the Bible.* **Sinaed** *packs it into her case. They leave.*

Bangles
— We made it across the ocean.
— Tiny bits of Indian sun hidden between cloth and fabric
— Between the words of God

Beat.

— In London, they find a home, but
— Hansa has to work in a factory
— Wearing grey clothes, trousers and blouses
— That tell her she doesn't belong
— Nothing like her saris
— She feels naked inside these tight clothes that show every part of her body
— So Hansa wears all of us – all six of us . . .
— A source of pride for where she has come from
— Golden sunshine that twinkles as she walks

London, 1975.

Sinaed   He's late again.

Hansa   He'll be back soon. Come, let's enjoy the silence before the men return.

Sinaed *rubs* **Hansa***'s shoulders.*

Sinaed   You have to take care – otherwise your arthritis will get worse . . .

Hansa   There's too much to do . . .

Sinaed   Let me – help you. You don't need to work anymore in the factory, Ma. I have enough from my new job.

Hansa   I can't sit at home and do nothing.

Sinaed   You can take care of the house – and maybe the new baby?

Hansa *smiles.*

Beat.

Hansa   Baby? About time!

Beat.

Once you asked me who Chandu is with you.

Sinaed   I remember.

Hansa   I want you to know – with you, he is a man, not a boy. With you – he is the man he wants to be.

Sinaed *smiles. They sit in silence. After a while,* **Hansa** *pulls off two* **Bangles**.

Hansa   These are for you . . .

Sinaed   Your bangles? No, I can't.

Hansa   Yes you can . . . And when I am gone – you will give these other four to your children.

Sinaed *hugs* **Hansa** *gently. She takes the* **Bangles** *and puts them on.*

London, present day.

Sinaed *gives* **Maya** *the* **Bangles**.

Maya   I am Maya: Sinaed and Chandu's daughter. After my grandmother died in 1993, my mum received the last four bangles from the set, and they were a bit thinner, since Ma wore them everyday.

On a special occasion, my mum gave my sister, Aru, and I both two.

I would wear them on special occasions, but about a year ago I had a hard time getting them off and decided I'll do as Ma did and keep them on.

I love the gentle sound they make, I love their timeless age, I love thinking of this bit of family history from India, Uganda, right to London, from grandmother to me, the next generation.

I carry them and this history with me everyday.

There is a line of women: **Hansa**, **Surya**, **Adhiti**, **Sinaed**, **Maya** *and* **Aru** *each wear their* **Bangles**.

Bangles
– We can't be taken off.
– Not without soap and hot water.
– We dance on Maya's wrists, long after her grandmother and mother pass.

Beat.

– When her daughter is born, Maya will put one aside for her.
– When her son marries, she will give one to the new groom
– For true love is always a little reckless and full of shine.

Scene Three: Immigration Office Bangles

Maya *stands in her spot behind the line.*

Crowd
– Take them off.
– Slip off those memories or
– You'll lose your place!
– Don't hold on!

Head Immigration Officer   Compelling I agree.
But the past will hold you back!
You must leave them here.
Or lose your chance of a future . . .

Maya   But, every time I move
They tinkle in my ear
Playing history's notes
Across my arms
Across my heart . . .

Joseph   We will need to make a choice, Maya. If we want a new life!

Maya   I know, I know – but /

Crowd (*escalating*)
– Shed or leave
– Integrate don't deviate . . .
– Be part of us.
– Not apart from us.

Crowd *tries to pull* **Bangles** *away from* **Maya.**

Crowd
– Shed or leave
– Integrate don't deviate . . .
– Be part of us.
– Not apart from us.

Crowd *tries to pull* **Bangles** *away from* **Maya**.

Joseph *stops them . . .*

Maya *holds onto* **Bangles** *. . .*

Head Immigration Officer   Hurry and decide.
Or we may change our mind!
Next!

Scene Four: Dog Tags

Several timelines as indicated.

Dog Tags
– First line, soldier's full name;
– Second line, serial number plus date of tetanus vaccinations and blood type;
– Third, fourth and fifth lines, address of next of kin and abbreviation for religion.

– I'm an oval-shaped stainless steel dog tag
– Identifier for the fighters
– For the ones that live
– But especially the ones that die.

– If my solider dies, they say a dog tag is placed between the teeth
– To prevent the body from gaseous bloating. . .!
– I wondered if it was true . . .
– I wondered what the stench of the dead would smell like
– And whether I would be afraid.

Beat.

– Jamaica, 1944.
– Second World War.
– Michael is twenty-five
– He joins the British Caribbean Division
– We sail for the Middle East
– We defend the borders
– Michael is thin and energetic.
– He wants to do his duty
– He believes in peace and equality . . .
– At night, when the others sleep
– Michael talks . . .
– He talks to his father, his mother
– But above all his wife and children
– Especially his children
– He tells his boys to be brave
– To fight for what they believe in
– Despite the dirt and lack of food
– Michael is a strong and loyal fighter
– Religious, full of faith and glory of God.
– Never left anyone without something in his stomach

– Even if it meant sharing what little he had.
– At night he would stroke the letters and numbers
– As if we were his key to getting home
– As he went to sleep he would tell himself that it wouldn't be much
   longer now.
– That he'd be going home soon . . .

Beat.

– Sadly, he was right.

Beat.

– An officer with a white coat and strong fingers cut me away from
   Michael's body.
– He recorded the letters and numbers.
– Breath and blood;
– The last of a life.
– Transcribed by pen and ink.
– They find a box and put me in there . . .
– Days later an officer with sad eyes picks me up.
– We meet Michael's wife Mary and three sons:
– William aged two, George aged four and Edward aged seven.

Officer   The Army sends it greatest condolences . . . I'm really
sorry . . . This was his . . .

Handing **Dog Tags** *to* **Mary.**

Mary   Thank you.

Dog Tags
– There is silence.
– I want to say something
– I want to tell them that when Michael was shot
– The last thing he thought of was the smiles of your faces
– I want to tell them that their father spent every night thinking of them
– That he missed their rowdy laughter and mischievous smiles.
– But I can't say anything.
– So I wait.
– Then there a warm hand, but softer and more curious.
– The smell of sweat like his father's, but fainter, sweeter.
– This is George.

A few years later.

*Three young boys (***William** *aged four,* **George** *aged six and* **Edward**
aged eight) playing with toy guns. **Edward** *shoots at* **William. William**
ducks, and the 'shot' then 'hits' **George.**

Edward   That got you.

William   No I ducked.

Edward   Not enough.

He walks around with his gun. **William** *is a little afraid.*

George   He ducked, Ed. I saw him.

Edward *points the gun at* **Joseph**.

Edward   I got you then.

George   No you didn't.

He stands up and confronts **Edward.**

Edward   I shot you.

George   You didn't shoot anything. It's not a real gun anyway.

Edward *gets up and goes closer to* **Joseph**. *He points the gun at his stomach.* **George** *is afraid.*

Edward   What's that?

He pulls at the **Dog Tags** *around* **George**'s *neck.*

George   Nothing.

Edward   Give it to me . . .

George   It was Father's.

Edward   So? Nobody cares what he did anyway. When I go to war, people will remember who I am.

George   Fighting doesn't solve anything.

Edward   Said who?

He comes closer, about to snatch the **Dog Tags** *away.* **George** *runs away.*

Dog Tags   He was right.
– Michael and his family never got anything after the war.
– Nothing except an empty space at the table and me.
– George hides me away, first in an old sock and later inside a box of
   books.
– He hides me away
– Hopes Edward will forget about me and going to war.
– But the pulse of the fight beats harder, louder in my brother
– What else is there for a boy like Edward to do?

– Fight a war, become a man
– In 1955 Edward decides to join the army – and be like his dad.
– He goes to fight for the British, during the Suez Crisis

Suez Crisis, Jamaica, 1965 – **William** *aged twenty-four,* **George** *aged twenty-five.*

Edward   It's time for me to go.

George   So go then.

Edward   I'm doing this for Father. For us.

George   And what about us? William, Mum and me?

Edward   I have to go.

Dog Tags   In the last moment, George gives in.
He finds me in the box

George   For good luck . . . See you when you get back.

Edward *and* **George** *hug.* **Edward** *puts the* **Dog Tags** *over his head.*

Dog Tags
– War: Stretches of earth burn under the sunlight.
– There is a lifeless village in the distance.
– The sweat on Edward's body, smells of loneliness and fear.
– There's explosion after explosion.
– Then one really loud gunshot.
– Edward is afraid
– He reaches deep into my pocket and pulls me out.
– Sits me around his neck
– The sweat begins to taste like hope
– He shoots back – strong and determined.
– Someone shouts 'Attack!' and starts firing.
– People fall.
– He looks around, desperate – not thinking.
– Acting on instinct.
– With a higher purpose.
– 'Retreat! Run back to cover'
– There is a deafening sound.
– Light all over.
– The earth hails down like heavy rain.
– But the only liquid I see are the pools of blood around us.

– Edward doesn't make it.
– After they identity his body, they find me also around his neck.

– They return me and the rest of his belongings
– Back to George
– George cleans me up, uses a soft cloth to gently ease away the dust and
  sand.
– He flattens one side which has become bent between two books.
– Then he begins to talk to me
– Just like his father did
– Telling me he wants something different for his children . . .
– For the future, not these numbers
– Not army, wars and death
– Education, opportunities and a chance to do something different.

George   Let's travel. Not for war this time.

William   Where? England? They don't want us!

George   Who cares? We fought their war!

William   That was Father, not us.

George   And our brother!
How many losses in this family.
For what?

William   We're not welcome

George   If we are good enough for their wars
We must be good enough for their streets
I need a change. A chance for a new life.

William   Then go. But I must stay – take care of Father's land and
Mama too.

George   Then take this.

He takes off one of the **Dog Tags** *and gives it to* **William***. The
brothers hug.*

Dog Tags
– George gives one of the tags to his brother.
– Keeps one half for himself.
– Finally, we travel again.
– This time – there are no guns or shootings.
– The dirty air is polluted, but not poisonous.
– The city is noisy but with cars, not bullets.
– It is dark and grey
– But somehow it feels bright and free.

Beat.

– Years later, when George has a little boy
– He prays that these numbers will lay to rest
– But as soon as he can, little Trevor
– Signs up to the army and goes to fight a war
– A war that was never needed
– A war that continued hate
– A war in someone else's name
– He took me along with him.

– But when he died
– I wasn't given to his son Joseph . . .
– His grandfather George keeps me
– He hopes his numbers will be different
– That life will cast a new spell
– And bring peace and new hope.

Scene Five: Immigration Office

Head Immigration Officer   Death and destruction . . . Those must be easy to give up . . .

Joseph *stands with the* **Dog Tags** *in his hand.*

Crowd   Give up! Give in!

Joseph   Sadness is easier to leave behind, Maya.

Maybe we should – just /

Head Immigration Officer   They are just objects.

They have no real value here . . .

Maya   But not all memories need to be good to be remembered, right?

Joseph   But to move forward, we have to let go, Maya.

Maya   I wish it was that easy!

Head Immigration Officer   You want in, you have to let go.

Joseph   Maybe we should just try to?

Head Immigration Officer   It's time to choose.

Immigration Officers   Before it's too late . . .

Crowd
– Shed or leave.
– Integrate don't deviate . . .
– Be part of us.
– Not apart from us . . .

Maya   We can't just walk away . . . As if they didn't mean anything

Joseph   But if we hold on – we'll never be able to move on. Have a new life, with opportunities . . .

Maya   That shouldn't mean we should forget who we are!

Joseph   Sometimes the memories are too painful.

Bangles   We remind you

Crowd   Shed or leave

Bangles   Of what you've become

Crowd   Integrate don't deviate

Dog Tags   Good can grow from difficulty

Crowd   Be part of us

Dog Tags   Dark from light

Crowd   Not apart from us

Maya   I'm not leaving this behind.
Good and bad.
It belongs to me.
To us!

She steps away from **Joseph.** *He tries to hold on to her but can't.*

River *and* **Skye** *wrap around her, protecting her from the crowd.*

Joseph *looks back at* **Dog Tags**, *about to step over the line.*

Bangles
– Keep growing
– Adding memories.
– Find strength
– In where you came from

Dog Tags
– So when you reach back
– You feel the strength
– Of the ones that came before you.

Bangles
– And even if you don't know
– Exactly who they were
– You know a part of you comes from them
– And a part of you will live on forever

Bangles   Wherever you go.
– Whatever you do.

Head Immigration Officer   Make your final choice. Decide who you are!

Joseph *looks at* **Maya**.

Maya   I'm golden sun *and* misty grey.

Joseph *goes back and claims* **Dog Tags** *and connects with* **Maya.**

Joseph   He was a *fighter*, but I'm a *pacifist* . . .

Maya *and* **Joseph**   We are both –

Bangles   The past . . .

Dog Tags   And the future!

River *and* Skye *address the crowd.*

River   The lines of a river change as the water erodes the ground

Skye
– Wherever you are in the world
– The sky is the same.

River   Movement is life . . .

Skye   In life
Change is inevitable . . .

River *and* **Skye** *begin to rub out the line.*

Skye   Our families have lived on the same soils for generations.
We retread their footsteps every day.

River   But – imagine living in a new place where you have no history.
No roots.

Maya   When you're moving generation after generation

Joseph   Where lives of loved ones are lost to power battles
Where your history leaves a bitter taste in your mouth

Skye   Stay here with us.
Use your history to plant new roots
And create new blooms.

Maya *and* **Joseph** *hold on to their keepsakes and go across to get through the 'Welcome' door.*

Skye *and* **River** *hold the crowd back.*

Keepsakes All
– As you journey forwards
– Let us mark the way.
– Form little clues
– To help others to find their way
– Back to family.
– Back to their homes
– Back to their hearts . . .

Potato Moon

Satinder Chohan

Author's Note

For *Potato Moon*, director Imogen Butler-Cole and I worked with a group of twenty-five Year 9 students at my former school, Villiers High in Southall. Located in a district of West London with a strong and proud migrant history, 90 per cent of Villiers students are first-generation immigrants, with only a few born in the UK. While Indians and Pakistanis comprise its largest groups, there has been an increase in students from Somalia, Afghanistan and Syria in recent years.

In the first of our two all-day workshops, Imogen and I used migration-themed drama games, scenarios, group improvisations and photographs (from the Migration Museum's *100 Images of Migration*) to develop character and story ideas for the short play. Student improvs featuring potatoes, a journey to the moon and a striking older female migrant who digs holes to stay calm later sprouted into the image and title of a 'potato moon' and the developing story of a young Southall girl who wants to migrate to the moon.

Researching and drafting, I discovered that as well as its own notable history of migration from South America to Europe, Asia and Africa over several centuries, the humble potato was the first vegetable to be grown in space in 1995. I also wanted to use the local allotments in Southall, where the potato is widely grown, as one of the play's settings. Many migrants, from former rural communities in Asia and Africa, use these small community patches of land to grow familiar vegetables from agricultural fields long left behind – digging up roots, planting new seeds.

Penning and polishing a script for the second workshop a month later, the students rehearsed all day and finished with a beautifully performed production for a Villiers audience.

A love letter of sorts to a migrant community enacted through their student children and grandchildren, *Potato Moon* digs into ideas around migration and memory as it celebrates a unique melting-pot community.

Characters

Mira
Bibi
Mum
Dad

Parakeets
The Trees
Seed Potato
Potatoes
The Trainspotters

Allotment Gang:
Mrs Kamaria
Mr Harith
Mr Ziemniak
Mrs Yahimba

Sunny's Gang:
Sunny
Bahdoon
Adnan
Logithan

Parakeets   Between the setting saffron sun
And a rising crescent moon,
We parakeets fly high above Southall town
One hazy late afternoon.
As the sun lowers its sweaty head for sleep,
The moon clips its sharp toenail sliver
On a nightly march across the starry sky,
Before it turns into a shiny silver sickle
Slicing through crops of cloud
That reveal Heathrow vapour trails
Scratching scars across the sky.
The sun drops its head low with a flaming flourish
Heating up Southall Castle, the old water tower
And its twin, the rotund blue gas tower,
Whose big LH letters and bright red lights
Welcome new arrivals still in flight.
Then standing like sentinels side by side,
The two towers cast long, dark shadows
Over Bibi's allotment nearby.
As the last sunset rays hit Sunrise Radio HQ,
Firing news of immigration raids across town
All the way into Mira's house
Back out through Sadia's house next door,
Radio waves pass sweet and spicy smells
Rising from the Noon Factory owned by the Curry King
Mingling with succulent Shahi Nan kebabs
And divine Sikh temple langhar food
In a mouthwatering Southall mix.
On railway tracks to and from London
Fast trains zip and steam trains rattle
While older ones from decades back
Stand brightly graffitied on abandoned tracks
'Sunny's Gang Woz Here'.

Mira stands above the trains
On the concrete bridge
Before she heads home after school.
Not for her any of this,
Nor the far-off pyramid Shard of red glass
The metropolis flickering in the distance
Or the steel Wembley Stadium arch
But a single upward stare –
She only has eyes for the moon.

She finally moves
Past the Afghan bazaar,
Twinkling with fabrics and jewellery,
Past the Somali cafes
Enticing with meat and vegetable stews,
Past the Polish vans
Filled with electrics and tools,
Slipping on split mangoes and okra
Tripping over coconuts
Chucked on the ground,
Shoved this way and that
By people rushing in and out of every grocers
Desperate to get their hands on an acute shortage of potatoes,
Bumping into people
Randomly stopping in the street,
Who are trying to remember
Faces
Names
People
And things
Because a veil of forgetfulness is falling over the town.
But Mira is oblivious to it all,
Just smiling back at the smiling moon
On her way home.

Mum and **Bibi** *open the door with tears in their eyes.*

Mum   Mira, there were raids on houses and shops round here.

Bibi   Our good neighbours the Omars were taken away.

Mira   Sadia too?

Mum   The whole family is being deported back home

Bibi   Because they don't have the right papers.

Mum   They've been told they can't stay here.

Parakeets   Mira tries to text her best friend.

Mira   'Where did they take u? R u ok?'

Parakeets   But her message is undelivered.
She pushes away a plate of pakoras
Deep fried with Bibi's prize veg
And takes a single sip from a cup of chai

Made with Bibi's healing masala, fennel and cardamom mix,
That does not soothe her troubled mind.

Mum   Let's watch some TV shall we?

Parakeets   Images of people in camps
Trudging deep in mud and dirt
In the freezing cold
Pushing across borders and rivers
Crammed into tiny boats adrift at sea
Children washed up dead on a beach.
Mira heads up to her room
Closing the door
Sits by the window
And weeps at the moon.

Dad *comes in soon after and holds* **Mira** *in his arms.*

Dad   We tried to reason with those men
But they wouldn't let the Omars go.
Sadia must go back to where she came from.

Mira   Will we too?

Dad   No, this is our home now for good.

Mira   Sadia thought so too.

Dad   Mira, we're here to stay.

Pause.

Mira   Dad, this world is too much to bear
When poor people can't move
From one place to the next
After we bomb their homes
Take away everything they have
Close down borders
Put up fences and walls
Shut down our hearts
Shut down our minds.
I want to move to the moon
Far away from it all.

Dad   Silly girl, you can't move to the moon,
Cos you've got to be a banker or doctor, innit?
Now wipe your tears, do your homework.
Come on now, get on with it.

Parakeets   Mira stares at her homework
But the tears continue to flow
Smudge the ink into one blurry whole.
In this way, the weeks pass
And Mira falls into a deep funk,
Without realising a deeper funk
In the town outside.
At school, she doesn't even notice when Sunny and his gang
shout:

Sunny/Adnan   Refugee kid, go back home!

Bahdoon/Logithan   Yeah, you parasite, leave us alone!

Parakeets   No point telling the teachers
Because they've forgotten her name
And everyone else's.
Can't remember their lessons either.
So Mira just hides her teary face in a book
Studies extra at school and extra at home
Working by the light of the moon.
Her family try to cheer her up
Showering her with treats.

Mum   It's your favourite – fish – but sorry no chips – from Britz!

Parakeets   Mira is about to tuck in
Pulling apart the greasy chip paper
When she sees black and white photos
Of migrants stuck at a border
Her tears mix with the salt and oil
And she runs away upstairs.

Bibi *hobbles after* **Mira** *with her walking stick and holds her tight.*

Mira   Bibi, why isn't this town doing more?
Sadia's gone, others will too.

Bibi   Puth*, there's something bigger afoot.
Come, I've something to show you.

Parakeets   Bibi and Mira take a long walk through the town
Where the veil of forgetfulness has grown into a shroud,
Till the silvery light of the moon

---

* 'My child' (Punjabi)

Threads together a patchwork of small gardens
And a place Mira had almost forgotten.

Mira   The allotment!
I'd chase butterflies and parakeets here.

Parakeets   Yes, us!

Mira   Build mudcastles in the soil
Pluck fruit from the plants
Dig up the veg.
But, Bibi, the fence has been torn down
Mounds of earth littered with broken bottles and cans
Shards of glass fill rows of holes
Big footprints have roughed up the earth.

Parakeets   Bibi nods her head.
In the shadow of the two towers
She draws Mira deeper into a secluded patch
Shielded by the most beautiful tall trees.

Mira   Bibi, where are we?

Bibi   The Memory Garden.

Mira   In memory of who?

Bibi   A memory garden for the whole town,
Every nation represented by us here in the allotment
Coming together from all over the world
To bury our painful memories
And keep our precious ones safe.
In this soil, our happy and sad memories
Grow warm, fill us with joy, heal us of pain,
Allowing news ones to grow.

Mira   Your memories grow in the earth?
Not inside your head?

Parakeets   Under her shawl
Bibi reaches into her pocket
Pulls out a misshapen vegetable with eyes
Roots hanging like little legs tugged from the ground.
Then as Bibi sparks her memory
The potato lights up in the palm of her hand.

Mira   Wow! Memories are potatoes?

Bibi   One of the last special seed potatoes here
With eyes and scars where the memories seep in
Of people and places we left far behind
Places we all once grew potatoes like these
Because potatoes have crossed vast oceans and land
Grown roots in every soil.
But a terrible fate has befallen this town
You've been so sad lately
You haven't noticed at all.

Mira   Noticed what?

Bibi   Mira, if we lose this seed potato,
We lose everything.

Parakeets   At that moment, The Trees bend in on Mira and Bibi,
Brushing leaves across their heads.
Mira turns to Bibi with a frightful stare.

Bibi   Don't worry, The Trees are our friends.

The Trees   Mira, your grandmother brought you here
Because our garden is full of empty holes
After someone broke in
Started stealing the town's memories.
So now our allotment members only remember

The **Allotment Gang** *steps forward.*

The Trees   Their time since they arrived here
Nothing before
Nothing about where they came from
Or how they got here.
There's Mrs Kamaria –

Mrs Kamaria   Why do I always feel this deep ache in my heart?

The Trees   There's Mr Harith –

Mr Harith   Why am I always digging holes when I get the chance?

The Trees   Mr Ziemniak –

Mr Ziemniak   Why do I always feel this burning hunger inside?

The Trees   Mrs Yahimba –

Mrs Yahimba   How did I get this heavy limp – and this bulletproof
Bible?

The Trees   Plus many more
Who have forgotten their way here.
Only Bibi's memory remains
Because the day that batch was stolen
From the next layer of memories down
We managed to scoop it up
Hid it in our leaves.

Bibi   I've dared not let this seed potato go,
In case we're also afflicted
Like the rest of our town
But we've got to plant it soon
Or a new batch of memories will be lost forever too.

She tucks the memory in her kameez pocket, under her shawl.

Mira   So the teachers forgetting their lessons?
Parents who can't remember their children's names?

The Trees   And all the others speaking only of now
Never of then
Because when they try talking of the past
There are only long silences
And emptiness within.

Allotment Gang   If we don't get those memories back soon
We'll forget the past forever,
Start forgetting the present too.
There will be nothing for us to hold on to.

The Trees   Mira, we all want to appoint you
Guardian of our Memory Garden.
Where we Trees are rooted to the earth
And your Bibi and Mum couldn't succeed,
We know you're young and quick enough
To catch the thief.

Mira   No, no, I'm not.

Bibi   Look at all these sad faces
Eaten away by loss.
What if you couldn't remember Sadia ever again?

Mira   Life might be better that way.

The Trees   That might be true but it would be a lie.
Whether life is happy or sad

A rollercoaster of memories
We need to strap in for the ride.
Because without both sun and rain,
Plants don't grow
Nor do our souls
Or our minds.

Bibi   If our town can't remember
Struggles of how our ancestors got here
Who'll stand up for Sadia
And others just like her?

The Trees   Mira, find out who did this criminal thing,
Bring back the memories lost,
So everyone can live in the present
And the future too.

The Trees/Allotment Gang   Do this for us
Help fill in the holes
And we promise to help you to get to the moon one day
If that is where you really wish to go.

———

Parakeets   The first night,
Mira keeps her eyes peeled to catch the thief
But by moonfall its hazy light
Lulls her into a sweet sleep.

The Trees   Mira, wake up! Wake up!
Not even The Trees can stop
The digging of memories from the deep.

The second night,
Mira runs tripwire low all around,
Upends a few tools to break the culprit's step
Fills a wheelbarrow with manure
For when the culprit falls flat on their face.
She hangs watering cans from a tree,
Filled with paint
Ready to shower and stain the thief.
But when she wakes the next day,
The wire has been snapped
A poor little rabbit was trapped
The paint chucked all around
And the last batch of deeply buried memories stolen.

The Trees   We tried to whip up a wind to blow the thieves away
But to no avail.

Mira   'Thieves'? What did they look like?

The Trees   Like humans.

Mira   Boys or girls?

The Trees   We don't know,
You all look the same to us.

The third night,
Mira sees Mum, Dad and Bibi's faces droop too low,
As their memory rot sets in.
For others, even though they have no past,
Their present is now being erased too.

Bibi *hands* **Mira** *the precious seed potato before she leaves.*

Bibi   We've waited as long as we can
But this must be planted tonight
Or a new generation of memories, including yours, will die.

As the strawberry full moon bleeds through the Memory
Garden,
Mira turns over Bibi's potato in her hand,
Its holes like the holes in the ruby-coloured moon
And plants it deep in the ground.
Basking in a rosy glow, Mira falls asleep,
But suddenly she's awoken when
The Trees sweep her head and the seed potato screams:

Seed Potato   Save me! Save me!

Parakeets   Mira sees Sunny and his Gang,
The school bullies
Stuffing Bibi's memory into a bulging bag,
Grabs a trowel and shakes it wildly at them.

Mira   Stop!

Sunny/Adnan   Refugee kid, go back home!

Bahdoon/Logithan   Yeah, you parasite, leave us alone!

Mira   Not till you hand over that bag.

Sunny   Like this town, it's ours, not yours!

Parakeets   Sunny and his gang dart from the allotment,
Mira chases in hot pursuit
All the way to Southall Station
Where The Trainspotters have gathered to see

The Trainspotters (*in nerdy voices*)   The historic steam train *The Moonflower*
Chugs its way towards the platform
To park up overnight,
With 1920s letters emblazoned on its side,
Posh dining carriages
And a roaring firebox steam oven.

Parakeets   That has caught Sunny's eye.

Parakeets/The Trainspotters   At the very moment Sunny and his gang
Run along the rickety bridge,
The train pumps out a huge cloud of steam
Bent out of shape by a flurry of coughs,
Lit up by electric flashes of light
From The Trainspotters trying to click a pic
Breaking into applause, whistles and cheers.
Sunny leaps over the bridge
Jumps onto the train
Engulfed in a huge cloud of smoke
And without a thought,
Mira jumps too.

Mira   Aaaaaaghhhhh!

Parakeets   Mira crawls on hands and knees,
Along the smoking top
Hot fumes cooking her face
Before Sunny drops into the train
And Mira follows him in.

The Trainspotters   He dashes through the ornate carriages
Cups and plates trembling
Chandelier lamps bopping and shaking
Old photos swinging in their frames,
Charging straight into the engine room

Parakeets   Where he opens up the firebox
About to tip out the bag,
Ready to roast the memories of the town.

Mira   Sunny, you can't steal what doesn't belong to you.

Sunny   Didn't you lot by coming here?
Taking my dad's job, then my mum's,
Taking a cheaper wage
Taking our homes
Crowding up our streets,
You freshies need to go back
Stop stealing from us.

Mira   Your parents and their parents
Generations before them
Came from somewhere else.
We're all in the same boat.

Sunny   We will be if I take these memories away
Then you will all be like me
No idea where I come from or why I'm here.
All of us one and the same.

Mira   Destroying someone's history
Is not the right thing to do.
Just because you don't know who you are
You'll stop everyone else knowing too?

Sunny   Swot, don't you pay attention in class?
'Whoever controls the past, controls the future too.'

Parakeets   Sunny rattles the bag, the potatoes shake and quiver.

Potatoes   Help! Keep us alive! Don't let us die!

Sunny   It's all in my hands now.

Mira   Sunny, there's no present and future without the past
Because our memories, good and bad, make us who we are.
Roast those memories
And you, me, all of us here, will just fade away
Lose everything that brought us all to our town.
Give me the bag and we'll help you grow
A past uniquely your own.
Then you'll see how much richer and deeper your life will be
When you realise you're not alone –
And you never have been.

She holds out her hand.

Parakeets   Sunny hesitates, while the gang outside urge him on.

Bahdoon/Adnan/Logithan   Spuds u roast!
Roast!
Roast!
Roast!

Sunny   It's true . . .
I feel alone.

Parakeets   Turning to his gang, Sunny says:

Sunny   You all do too.
Don't know who we are
Or why we're here . . .
Mira, you'll help us figure it out, you swear?

Mira   I swear.

Sunny *lowers the bag, then hands it to* **Mira**.

Parakeets   Outside the train,
Mum, Dad, Bibi, the Allotment Gang's and other faces
Are turning completely blank,
So Mira quickly opens the carriage door
Casting memories to everyone.
One by one, they hold the potatoes
And the past and present glow in their hands.

Mrs Kamaria   Bahdoon, is that you, my son?

Bahdoon   Mum?

Parakeets   Mrs Kamaria spots her son
Long lost crossing the Somali border.
With a tearful embrace,
The ache in her heart immediately stops
While applause breaks out all around.
Seeing this, Mr Harith makes a vow:

Mr Harith   I used to dig for oil
Then dug graves for my family
Killed by bombs in Kabul.
Now I'll stop digging holes to stay calm
Fill the lives of my newborn baby
And those I love again.

Adnan   If you're retiring, can I have your spade?

Parakeets   Mr Ziemniak's memory lights up

And so do his eyes.
Old family recipes whisper their way
Back into his mind.

Mr Ziemniak   I'll grow the biggest potatoes here,
To make and sell Grandpa's smooth and creamy potato vodkas
And Grandma's famous Polish potato salads.

Logithan   I love potato salad!

Mr Ziemniak   I'll teach you how to make it if you like.

Logithan   Cool!

Parakeets   Mrs Yahimba raises her hands
And bulletproof Bible in the air:

Mrs Yahimba   Praise be to Jesus!
I got this limp flying from Nairobi to London
Curled up tight in the nose wheel of the plane.
Wedged in by my soldier mother's bulletproof Bible,
Which stopped me dropping from the skies
And battled the icy winds.

Mum *and* **Dad** *hug and kiss* **Mira**.

Mum *and* **Dad**   We're happy because we've got our old Mira back.

Smiling proudly, **Bibi** *holds out the seed potato for* **Mira**.

Bibi   Puth, you know what to do.

Parakeets   Mira places the potato in the palm of Sunny's hand.

Mira   Close your eyes.
Hold this close to your heart.

Parakeets   Sunny holds the potato, as it lights up.

Sunny   I can see a tall turbaned man,
Diamonds in his beard and a gun in his hand,
Fighting in British Army uniform
In a faraway land . . .

Parakeets   Mira looks up and smiles at the rosy-cheeked full moon
And knows that one day
Like so many others
She needs to move away too.

———

Parakeets   Bibi and the Allotment Gang work their green fingers,
Bringing together expert gardening skills,
Love
And conversation,
To grow The Trees taller
Than even The Trees ever thought they could be.
Soaring higher than Southall Castle
And the gas tower
Many hundreds of times combined
The Trees break through clouds
Thick with sweet and spicy smells
To lift Mira up,
All the way to the moon.

In her DIY mobile space capsule
Parked up by the Lake of Dreams,
After long stints by the Lake of Forgetfulness
And the Lake of Time,
Mira crunches around in her silver bling spacesuit
Watching a beautiful sea-blue Earthrise in the black sky
A bindi dot Sun in starry space behind.
But today is extra special –
It's Diwali
Eid
And Guy Fawkes
On the very same day.
Mira picks up a small embroidered pouch
Lifts the hatch and steps out of the capsule
Touching her moonboots onto the rocky surface.
She takes out the seed potato Bibi gave her when she left
Placing it with love deep in a crater
Cups moondust in her gloved hands
Sprinkling it all over
In her new Memory Garden on the moon.

Suddenly, dhol and batar drums beat
From far far away.
Mira turns towards Earth all aglow
Candles burning
Rainbow fireworks exploding
Green crescent moon and orange khanda flags flying
Brightly dressed people from all over
Meeting

Feasting
Dancing
In one pulsating place,
Where tall trees sway
And is that Sadia sending her a wave?
Mira peers more closely –
Southall!
A single tear falls
Slips out of her helmet
Drops into the crater
Growing a shoot
That roots deep in the moon
And fills her
With a deep longing for . . .

Mira   Home.

Willkommen

Asif Khan

Author's Note

I was approached by Fin Kennedy from Tamasha Theatre Company, who kindly asked if I would like to take part in a new project in conjunction with the Migration Museum. Teamed with director Esther Richardson, the project involved both of us working with Drama students from Landau Forte College (Derby). The students had various levels of ability and experience, but were all enthusiastic about the project.

During our first day with them, we used various devising exercises to generate potential story ideas, characters and material on the subject of migration. I then took this away and used it to write a thirty-minute play for them. During our second day, Esther rehearsed the students in preparation for a script-in-hand performance of the play, which they gave to their peers on that same day.

This was my first theatre-writing commission and naturally I learned a great deal in the process. I had to ensure the play would interest and connect with the students, provide each of them a role to play, be no more than thirty minutes in length and also be suitable enough for them to perform it as a script-in-hand performance after only a few hours' rehearsal with minimal props. It was also important to incorporate the ideas they generated in the first-day workshop, so the students felt the play was not only written specifically for them, but also that they had a part to play in its writing.

It was hugely rewarding to see their performance of the play and I was so impressed with how much they had absorbed during the few hours' rehearsal with Esther.

Characters

Speaking roles:

Ammar, *nine years old, central character and narrator. He can be played by one actor throughout or by a different actor in each section (male or female). He wears a baseball cap (or backpack), which could be passed from actor to actor to identify him easily, if he is being played by more than one person.*

Papa
Mama
Smuggler 1
Smuggler 2
Boatman
Boatwoman
Dream Voice 1
Dream Voice 2
Houda
Taxi Driver
Man by Fence 1
Police 1
Police 2
Woman by Fence 1
Woman by Fence 2
Man by Fence 2
Tennis Player
Cameraman
Man with Megaphone
Train Station Man
Train Station Woman 1
Crowd 1
Crowd 2
Train Station Woman 2
Mahmoud
Camerawoman
Car Woman
Motorway Man
Man in Suit
Motorway Woman
Refugee 1
Refugee 2
Refugee 3

Triceratops
Interviewer
Houda's Mother
Train Driver
Crowd 3

Possible non-speaking roles:

Ammar's Auntie
Ammar's Sister, three years old
Fisherman
Motorway Drivers

Notes on casting: The director of the piece is free to cast as they wish depending on the cast size and split roles further if necessary. I have also made suggestions about where this could be done throughout the script. There are also some roles that are not gender-specific, such as Smuggler, Police, Refugee, Taxi Driver and Dream Voice. These can be played by male or female actors.

Scene One: The Final Day

Papa   Please help us!
The regime is killing us!
Everyday there is blood!
I can't speak!
Please help us!

Ammar   I heard my papa scream this on my final day in my home country
He screamed this to a man with a camera
Surrounding him were lots of my people
All watching
Some crying
As a woman lay bleeding on the floor
This woman was my auntie Sofia
Papa's sister

Papa   Why won't they help us?!

Ammar
I had got used to the sound of bombs
I had got used to the sound of guns
I had got used to the sound of screaming
Many days
Weeks
Months
Had I slept through this
But
One thing I was not used to
One thing I had never seen
Was the sound
And sight
Of Papa crying
Tears running down his cheeks
Crying like my little sister
I was not used to this
This is what woke me
On my final day in my home country

I crawled back under my blanket
Where I felt safe
I stayed there
As I heard Papa

Back in my house
Saying to my mother

Papa   That's it!
No more!
No more!

Ammar   Mama touched my cheek
Kissed my forehead

Mama   Wake up, my darling Ammar
Collect all your clothes
Collect all your colouring pens
We have to go from here

Ammar   Where, Mama?
Where?

Mama   I don't know, Ammar
I don't know

Scene Two: The Boat

Ammar   Ten
Twenty
Forty
A hundred
People arrived on the beach
Hiding in bushes
For a whole night
Waiting
To get on
I held Papa's hand
Tight
As men
With guns
Shouting words I couldn't understand
Ordered people
When will we get on the boat, Papa?

Papa   Ssh, Ammar

Ammar   Then
A boat

Smugglers *can be separated further between more actors depending on*
cast size.

Smuggler 1   You, you and you back!
Everybody in front, go!
Women, children first!

Ammar   Mama took us to the boat
It was filling up
Children crying
I couldn't see the beach
I couldn't see my papa
There were too many people
I was worried
There would be no room

Smuggler 2   Right, go!

Ammar   Then
Splash!
As the men
Race towards the boat
To join their families
Mama gripped my hand
The boat shook
As the men climbed in
Water splashing inside
I couldn't see him
So many people
We lost him!
Then
Papa's hand
On my chest
Pulling me towards him
He made it!

Smuggler 2   You! Off!

Ammar   My father hides inside the boat
BANG!
He shoots the clouds

Smuggler 2 *grabs* **Papa** *and pulls him off the boat.*

Smuggler 2   Push or nobody leaves!

Ammar   The engine starts

Slowly at first
Then faster
Smoke fills the air
It makes me cough
Papa pushes
We begin to move
Faster
And faster
Then
Splash!
Papa slips
Falls into the water
The distance
Gets bigger
And bigger
Papa!

Mama   Quick! Faster!

Ammar   Papa swims
Arms flapping
Battling the waves
He's not going to make it, Mama!

Mama   Faster! Come on!

Ammar   Others shout
Faster! Faster!
A man
Stretches out his arm
Grabs my father
Pulls him
Back onto the boat
Safe
Thank you, God!
Wet
Breathless
He wraps his arms around us all

The boat continues
Engine
Struggling
Smoke
Black smoke

Smell of petrol
Some cry
Some pray
Some are silent
All crammed
Squashed
Swinging
Left and right

Boatman   Don't go too fast!
Go slowly if it means we arrive safely

Ammar   Night falls
It gets darker
Colder
All I can see is black
Apart from the light of phones
The smoke continues
The engine struggles
What if it stops?
I couldn't breathe
Mama wraps a scarf around my face
My sister's face
Then
The engine
Gets slower
And slower
Until

Silence

Whistles
People blow whistles on their jackets
Wave the light from their phones
Moving
Waving
Moving

Boatman   Everyone stop moving or we're going to capsize!

Ammar   My heart races

Boatwoman   They're going to come, but it takes time

Boatman   A lot of people die here, so everyone is scared

Ammar   Hours pass
Then
In the distance
In the darkness
A light
Gets bigger
A boat
A fisherman!

Boatman *and* **Boatwoman**   Over here! Come to here!

Ammar   The fisherman throws a rope
We're safe!
We see lights
Land
People cheer
Clap
Cry
Hug
And thank God
The sea is very scary, Papa

Scene Three: The Island

Ammar   Pebbles
Stones
Sand
A shell
Beneath my feet
Out there
The water
The waves
We left behind
Are we here, Papa?

Papa   No, Ammar

Ammar   How long, Papa?

Silence.

Ammar   How long, Papa?

Papa   Soon, Ammar

Ammar   More boats
Crammed
With families
Relief
Prayers
And tears
Papa lays a blanket on the floor

Papa   Here, come
Rest
Sleep

Ammar *sleeps.*

Ammar   I'm on the water
Back on the boat
Just me
And the sea
The waves are calm
The sun is sinking
Where is my family?
How did I get here?
Why am I by myself?
I'm not scared
But then
The waves
Begin to swing the boat
Two huge hands
As huge as me
Come out of the sea
Papa's hands?
They look like his
They tickle me
Yes it's Papa!
Stop it, Papa!
You're tickling me!
Stop it, Papa!
You're hurting me!
You're hurting me, Papa!!
Whoof!
They pick me up
High above the boat
Then
Whoof!

They bring me down
Into the water

Dream Voices *can be separated further between more actors depending
on cast size.*

Dream Voice 1   You're going to die in the water

Dream Voice 2   We don't want you

Dream Voice 1   You're going to die in the water

Dream Voice 2   We don't need you

Dream Voice 1   You're going to die in the water

Dream Voice 2   We don't like you

Ammar   I can't breathe!

A series of deep breaths. **Ammar** *wakes up.*

Papa   Ammar, it's ok

Ammar   Papa?

Papa   It's ok
Bad dream

Ammar   It's bright
The sun is shining
We're on the beach
Clothes are drying
People are chatting
Some catch fish
Mama is packing

Houda   Hello

Ammar   Hello

Houda   What's your name?

Ammar   Ammar. What's yours?

Houda   Houda. Is that your family?

Ammar   Yes. Where are yours?

Houda   My mum is over there drying my dress

Ammar   Oh

Houda   Where are you going?

Ammar   I don't know
But my mama said it will be safe
No bombs
And there will be schools
Where I can paint
Where I can make new friends

Houda   That might be where I'm going

Ammar   Where are you going?

Houda   A place
Where it will be safe
No bombs
Where they'll be schools
Where I can read
Where I can make new friends

Ammar   It must be the same place!

Houda   Mama said
That when we arrive
The people will shout
Willkommen!

Ammar   What does that mean?

Houda   Welcome!

Papa   Ammar!

Ammar   I better go.
Roads
Cars
Motorbikes
Lorries
Lots of people
A man selling necklaces
Another selling water
The smell
Of cooking
I don't know what
But it made me hungrier
Papa shouted

Papa   Taxi!

Taxi Driver   Yes

Papa   To the north of the island

Taxi Driver   I cannot take, my friend

Papa   Why?

Taxi Driver   Not allowed to take your people

Papa   I pay you good money

Taxi Driver   I'm sorry, friend
Cannot take
Against the law
You get sent to the court
They take my licence

Ammar   We started walking
It was hot
Sun was pounding
Many
Behind me
Many
In front
Children
Mothers
Fathers
Grandfathers
The roads get longer
And longer
My feet hurt, Papa

Papa   Not long, Ammar
Soon we'll be on a boat

Ammar   I don't want to go on a boat again

Papa   This time
It will be different
Safer
It's a big boat
A ferry

Ammar   Papa picks me up
On his back

We continue
Walking
I hear Papa panting
He must be tired too
Sweat drips from his hair
On to my arms
I imagine I'm riding on an elephant
No
A dinosaur!
A Triceratops
Finally

Papa   Let's rest here

Ammar   My sister is crying
Mama rocks her to sleep
Papa buys water and bananas
We sit on rocks
Under a tree
Hiding from the sun

Houda   Ammar!

Ammar   It's Houda and her mother!

Houda   Do you want some orange?

She tears off some and gives it to **Ammar**.

Ammar   Shall we play a game?

Houda   What kind?

Ammar *takes out pens and a sketchbook.*

Ammar   What am I drawing?

Houda   A cow!

Ammar   No

Houda   A bull?

Ammar   No

Houda   What is it?

Ammar   You have to guess!

Houda   Is it a dinosaur?

Ammar   What kind?

Houda   I don't know

Ammar   A Triceratops!
It's my favourite dinosaur
It has three huge horns
And a shell around its neck
It's gentle
But when it gets attacked
By a T-Rex
It uses its horns
To fight back!
You have a go

Houda *draws.* **Ammar** *tries to guess. This can be improvised and the*
actors can decide what **Houda** *draws and how easily* **Ammar** *guesses,*
e.g. elephant, ship, soldier, flower. It could be represented physically, i.e.
the characters move and position various members of the ensemble to
create a still picture of their drawing.

Papa   Ammar!

Ammar   I have to go

Houda   Maybe I'll see you later on?

Ammar   Papa said we're going to a big ferry
Maybe I'll see you there?

Houda   We could play more on the ferry

Ammar *leaves* **Houda**.

Ammar   We walk
Hours pass by
Finally
I can see it, Papa!
We arrive
At the big ferry
It's much bigger
And taller than I thought!
Tents fill the empty car park
Many people
All waiting to get on
Papa finds an empty tent

Papa   In here
It's raining

Let's sleep
Tomorrow
We get on the big boat

Ammar *sleeps.*

Dream Voice 1   You're all alone

Dream Voice 2   No one wants you

Dream Voice 1   Go away

Dream Voice 2   You're worthless

Ammar   Why?

Dream Voice 1   You don't belong here

Dream Voice 2   Get back on the boat

Dream Voice 1   You took all our houses

Dream Voice 2   Get back on the boat

Dream Voice 1   You took all our money

Dream Voice 2   Get back on the boat

Ammar   I didn't!

Dream Voice 1   It's all your fault

Dream Voice 2   It's all your fault

Dream Voice 1 *and* **2**   It's. All. Your. Fault!

Ammar   STOP!

Scene Four: The Fence

Ammar   A metal fence
Taller than a house
Circles and circles
Of prickly wire
It's been days
Hundreds of my people
Blocked
Thinking the same
What do we do now?
Papa approaches a man

Papa   How long is this fence?

Man by Fence 1   A hundred miles
They knew we were coming
This is what they build
They treat us like animals

Papa   How long have you been here?

Man by Fence 1   Nine long days
Nine cold nights
My daughter's not eaten since yesterday
When did you arrive?

Papa   Five days ago

Police 1   Move! Move away!

Ammar   Shout policemen

Police 2   Go back! Move away!

Man by Fence 1   We are fleeing a war!
We haven't come here to steal your lives

Ammar   A crowd begins to gather
At the centre
A small girl

Woman by Fence 1   What's happened?

Woman by Fence 2   She's passed out

Woman by Fence 1   Keep her warm

Man by Fence 2   Look at the situation here
These are just children
If we didn't die there
We'll die here
Next to this fence

Ammar   They take the girl away
(*To* **Mama**.) I hope she's going to be ok, Mama
I see a boy speaking to a camera

Tennis Player   My tennis career started when I was seven years old
And ended when I was sixteen years old
Last year
Because of the problems there

And now I plan to continue my career
Over there
If they let me go

Ammar   A woman speaks to another camera

Women by Fence 1   There was a missile
It killed twelve people
That day we decided we should leave

Cameraman   People here are angry and nervous about their country
Accepting so many of you
Can you understand why?

Women by Fence 1   Maybe some radical type of people come to their
    country
But we are not them
They are not us
I have a message for them
You already know we come out of a place of death
We don't want to go to another death

Ammar   Then
A police car
Drives into the crowd
A man with a megaphone shouts

Man with Megaphone   The police are saying they are going to clear
the area
They've just requested tear gas
They say you should register in the camp
And when you register in the camp
Maybe they will help you after that
These are the words of the police
Not mine
I'm transmitting the police's message
I'm doing it for you
So they do not harm you

Man by Fence 2   What choice do we have?
The police will put the gas in my face
Also my family
They force us

Ammar   As people start to gather their things

Man by Fence 1   Quick! Run!

Ammar   People begin to escape through a hole in the fence!

Papa   Run!

They all run.

Ammar   Shouting
Gunshots
Screams
Then

Papa *holding* **Ammar** *trips.* **Papa** *lands on* **Ammar**.

Ammar   Aaaaahhhhh!

Papa   Ammar!

Ammar   My arm, Papa!

Police 2 *grabs* **Papa** *by his collar.* **Papa** *pushes him to the ground.*

Police 2   You rat!
You filthy animal!

Ammar   Papa runs
I hold him tight
My arm in pain
Hundreds run
In the same direction
To the fence
To the hole in the fence
To the other side
And run
And run
Where they can't reach us
And run
And run
And run
Where we're free!

Scene Five: The Train Station

Ammar's *asleep.*

Dream Voice 1   No one wants you

Dream Voice 2   You're worthless

Dream Voice 1   You're a filthy animal

Dream Voice 2   You're a rat

Ammar   Why?

Dream Voice 2   You don't belong here

Dream Voice 1   Get back on the boat

Dream Voice 2   You took all our houses

Dream Voice 1   Get back on the boat

Dream Voice 2   You took all our money

Dream Voice 1   Get back on the boat, *rat*!

Ammar   Don't call me that

Dream Voice 1   It's all your fault, rat

Dream Voice 2   It's all your fault, rat

Dream Voice 1 *and* **2**   It's. All. Your. Fault. RAT!

Ammar *wakes up.*

Ammar   I'm sweating
It's morning
We're at the train station
Still waiting for the train
Which will take us
Where we want to be
The place where people will accept us
The place where we'll be able to build a new life
The place where
They'll all shout
Willkommen!
Here, however
A man shouts

Train Station Man   My family and children have no more money to eat
Drink water at least
We have no more words to describe our situation
What is the definition of being a refugee?
To be treated like dirt?
To be living and sleeping on the ground?

Ammar   When will they let us on the train, Mama?

Mama   Soon, Ammar

Ammar   Why are they so cruel to us?

Mama   The leaders here are cruel
They're the ones who closed the train station
But the people here are kind
Look
Yesterday
They gave us blankets

Ammar   On a big screen
Above the square
A woman
Wearing a blue suit
Speaks at a stand
Mama watches
Papa watches
Everyone watches

Ammar   Who is that woman, Mama?

Mama   It's the leader of the country we will live in

Ammar *listens with everyone else.*

Prime Minister   It is estimated nine million have fled their homes
That figure alone shows what the size of the issue is
We have to protect those fleeing war
Fleeing persecution
To those coming
We expect them to integrate into our societies
And learn our language
But we have a duty to stand by them with respect
To see them as people

Ammar   Will it be hard to learn their language, Mama?

Mama   It will take time
But there are schools
And you will be with others like you
You will learn together

Ammar   I know one word already, Mama

Mama   What's that, Ammar?

Ammar   '*Willkommen*'

It means 'welcome'!
I met a friend
Who said when we arrive
They will all shout this word

Mama   I'll be happy if I hear that word

Ammar   Can I have my pens, Mama?

Mama *takes out* **Ammar***'s pens. The following could be represented theatrically as before, using the ensemble.*

Ammar   I draw a picture of me
My mama, papa and my sister
With our bags
Arriving
And crowds
Big crowds of people
Saying
This word

Train Station Woman 1   What are you drawing?

Ammar   I'm drawing what we're going to see

Train Station Woman 1   You're very talented

Ammar   I like to draw
And paint
When I grow up
I want to have my paintings in museums
Like Leonardo
And Michelangelo
So people can see them

Train Station Woman 1   I'm sure many people will want to see them

Crowd 1   We want to go! We want to go!

Ammar   Shouts a man
Others join

Crowd 1   We want to go! We want to go!

Ammar   More join

Crowd 1   We want to go! We want to go!

Ammar   Until everyone around me joins

Crowd 1   We want to go! WE WANT TO GO!

Ammar   They keep chanting
For hours
Then
I hear a different crowd
A different chant

Crowd 2   Go away, we don't want you! Go away, we don't want you!

Ammar   They look angry

Crowd 2   Go away, we don't want you! Go away, we don't want you!

Train Station Woman 2   You should be ashamed of yourselves
You're an embarrassment to this country!

Ammar   Shouts an old woman

Train Station Woman 2   What if you were desperate?!
What if you were fleeing war?!

Crowd 2   Go away, we don't want you! Go away, we don't want you!

Train Station Woman 2   Why don't they open the station?
Why don't they let them leave?

The following chants repeat and could be overlapped to create the chaos and anger of the crowds.

Crowd 2   Go away, we don't want you! Go away, we don't want you!

Crowd 1   We want to go! We want to go!

Ammar   Then some of the crowd
With sticks
And bats
Charge into us
Police run in
And the angry crowds
Get angrier
Papa picks me up
Protects Mama
And my sister
Moves us away
Soon
More police
More sirens
An ambulance

A fire engine
A man with a hose
Fires water

Police 1   Move back!

Ammar   The water is strong
In one blast
It pushes many of the crowd over
Some try to run through
Second blast!
It pushes them over
Some decide
It's not worth it
And move back
(*To* **Papa**.) They must really hate us, Papa

Papa   There are good people too
For every bad human being
You will find three good human beings

Scene Six: The Long Walk

Train Station Man   You don't open the station, we walk!

Ammar   Shouts a man

Train Station Man   Guys, we are walking! We have nothing here!

Ammar   They start to move away from the station
Towards the big road
Many others follow

Papa   Come on, let's go

Mama   It's miles and miles

Papa   It doesn't matter
As long as we're getting closer
Anything is better than waiting
Hoping
For a train that may
Or may never come
This will shame their leader
This will shame their country
For not helping us

I've had enough of sleeping on the street
With the children in the cold

Ammar   We start to walk
People cheer

Crowd 1   We're walking!
We're walking!

We see **Mahmoud** *walk past* **Ammar**.

Mahmoud   We want to get there because we will get our rights

Ammar   Says a man on crutches
Camerawomen and reporters
Follow him

Camerawoman   Do you know how many kilometres it is?

Mahmoud (*smiling*)   I don't know, but we are walking!

Camerawoman   What's your name?

Mahmoud   Mahmoud

Camerawoman   What happened to your leg?

Mahmoud   It was injured in the war
I have one real leg
One plastic leg
And one heart
Telling me to walk

Camerawoman   Do you really think you can get there with one leg?

Mahmoud (*smiling*)   Yes I will, my friend

Ammar   As we continue
Cars and lorries
Fly by
We pass over a bridge
Over a huge river

Mama   It's beautiful

Ammar   Says Mama
I could see buildings
Houses
Signs
Writing

A different language
Trees
So green
Not brown and sandy
Like home
In the distance
Mountains
Everybody was looking out
Smiling and cheering
We were tired
But happy
However long it takes
We would be ok
We were on our way
Together
Supporting each other
It was like we were in a film
A film with a happy ending
We move onto a busy motorway
Cars whizz by
Some open their windows
Spit at us
Shout at us
I don't know what
But I know it's something bad
I keep my head down
Then
A woman pulls over and steps out

Car Woman   This is your family?

Papa   Yes this is my family

Car Woman   If you want, you can come in our car

Papa   Those are my people
I am like them
I will walk like them
It's ok
We will walk
And what will happen to them
Will happen to me

Car Woman   I'm just worried about the children

Papa   There are so many children
My children are no better than those children

Car Woman   Are you sure?

Papa   When war was in our neighbour's country
We received a lot of people
We put them in our houses
We don't treat them like refugees
We treat them like brothers
But when war was in *my* country
Most of us lost our schools
Our jobs
We lost our identity even
And the world was silent
But there are some good people
You are a good person
But we have to stick together

Motorway Man   There's a resting point just after the bridge
There are cars handing out water

Ammar   Shouts a man
Some local people
Stand by crates
Hand out bottles of water
I'm so thirsty
I see a man in a suit handing out water
Talking to a cameraman

Man in Suit   I was stuck in the traffic jam
And I looked in my mirror
And I saw something
I've never seen before
Thousands of people
I'm not really this kind of person
This is the first time in my life I've helped anyone

Ammar   A woman comes forward

Motorway Woman   It is very important for people to realise
That what our government is doing
They are not doing in our names
Come get your bottle of water!

Ammar   Everybody sits

At the side of the road
Resting their feet
Drinking
Then
I see the man with one leg
I see Mahmoud!
He's on the back of a bicycle
Holding his crutches
As a man rides him up the road

Mahmoud   This is a good man!

Ammar   The journey continues
My feet begin to hurt
Really hurt
I can't walk without limping
Each step is painful
I wish I didn't have to walk
I really wish I didn't
But I have to
Even though I feel like crying
I have to be strong
I have to be a man
Like Papa
Mama's feet begin to bleed
Papa takes off his shoes
Gives them to Mama
And wears her shoes

Ammar   You look funny, Papa!

Papa   Now you have two mothers!

Ammar *and* **Mama** *laugh.*

Papa   To be or not to be
That is the question
We will be!

Ammar   We will be!
Hours and hours
Night begins to fall
I can no longer feel my feet
People begin to gather at the side of the road
On the open grass
Then

Ammar   Auntie Sophia!

Papa   What, Ammar?

Ammar   There's Auntie Sophia!

Papa   Auntie Sophia is dead, Ammar

He kisses **Ammar**'s *head.*

Ammar   Papa look
Big field
Ours

Papa   Let's sleep.
(*Joking.*) Which room would you like?

Ammar *and* **Mama** *laugh.*

They all hug each other and sit on the grass.

Ammar   My feet really hurt, Papa.

Papa   Here, take them off

Ammar   He massages my feet
They begin to feel better
I begin to feel tired
So tired

Ammar *falls asleep.*

Dream Voice 1   No one wants you

Dream Voice 2   You're worthless

Dream Voice 1   You're a filthy animal

Dream Voice 2   You're a rat

Ammar   No!

Dream Voice 1   You don't belong here

Dream Voice 2   Get back on the boat

Dream Voice 1   You took all our houses

Dream Voice 2   Get back on the boat

Dream Voice 1   You took all our money

Dream Voice 2   Get back on the boat, *rat*!

Ammar   Don't call me that!

Dream Voice 2   Carry on walking

Dream Voice 1   You'll be walking

Dream Voice 2   And walking

Dream Voice 1   Forever!

Dream Voice 1 *throws something at* **Ammar**. **Ammar** *wakes up.*

Ammar   On my chest
I see a broken egg
Its contents
All over my body
Papa gets up
Shouts after a car

Papa   You evil people!

Mama *takes out a tissue and wipes* **Ammar**'s *clothes.*

Refugee 1   We have some good news!

Ammar   A man shouts

Refugee 1   We have won a huge victory!

Refugee 2   What?

Refugee 1   They are sending buses!
They've been shamed!

Refugee 2   Wait!
I don't trust these buses
What if they takes us in the wrong direction?
Where is the guarantee?
There's no media here
They're lying
We've made it a third of the way
Forty kilometres
There's not that much further to go
We must stick together

Ammar   The men talk
Argue
Finally

Refugee 1   Let's send the first bus ahead
And then wait to hear back from the border
If everything is ok
The rest will follow

Police 1   You don't trust me?

Refugee 1   I know my people
I know how they're thinking

Ammar   Silence
A few hours
We all wait
Anticipating
Hoping
We hear some good news
Finally

Refugee 1   Listen, everybody!
Can you tell these people where you are?
I've got you on loudspeaker

Refugee 3   We're nearly at the border
I'm following our route on my phone
It's 100 per cent right

Refugee 1   Thank you so much for letting us know

Everyone cheers, claps and hugs each other.

Ammar   The buses arrive
Fifty people get on
Fifty people go
Another bus arrives
Fifty people get on
Fifty people go
And so on
Until we reach the front of the queue
And finally we get on
The seats are comfortable
So comfortable

Ammar *falls asleep.*

Dream Voice 1   You're a filthy animal

Dream Voice 2   You're a rat!

Ammar   Don't call me that!

Dream Voice 1   Nobody wants you

Dream Voice 2   Go away

Dream Voice 1   Nobody wants you

Dream Voice 2   Get lost

Triceratops   Don't listen to them

Ammar   It's a Triceratops!
Are you a real Triceratops?

Triceratops   I am, Ammar

Ammar   How do you know my name?

Triceratops   I've heard of you
And your brilliant paintings
Everybody has
I've wanted to meet you for a long time

Ammar   Really?

Dream Voice 1   Nobody wants you!

Dream Voice 2   Go away!

Dream Voice 1   Nobody wants you!

Dream Voice 2   Get lost!

Triceratops   Let me take care of this

The **Triceratops** *fights off* **Dream Voice 1 and 2** *and defeats them.*

Ammar   Thanks, Triceratops!

Triceratops   *Willkommen*
Willkommen
Willkommen

Ammar *wakes up.*

Ammar   It's daylight
We're not on the bus anymore
But on a train
When did we get on a train?
How long was I asleep?
It must have been a long time!
Papa is talking to a man with a microphone

Papa   We are peaceful, my people
We are hard workers
We are educated
We love each other
We share our blankets
We share our food
We share our shoes
I would do the same with you
If you were in my position
There is no difference between us
So don't be afraid of us
We are human just like you
We don't have weapons
Just our legs

Interviewer   How do you feel now that you're almost there?

Papa   We have reason again to hope
We want a good life for our children
We make it to the final train
To take us to our new home

Ammar   Then
I see Houda's mother!
Peace be upon you!

Houda's Mother   Peace be upon you too
How are you?

Ammar   Excited
Where's Houda?
I've got lots to tell her

Houda's Mother   I'm afraid
She isn't here anymore

Ammar   Where is she?

No response.

She didn't need to answer
Her eyes said it all
As they filled with tears
I couldn't speak

Ammar *hugs her.*

(*To audience.*) She was almost there
She almost made it
She didn't get to hear the crowd shout
Willkommen
When I get to my new home
I'm going to paint a picture
For Houda
Of what she came so close to seeing
Of what she could have seen
The final part of the journey
The final part of the story
The final part she missed out on

Scene Seven: The Willkommen

Train Driver   Ladies and gentlemen
We are now arriving at our final destination

Ammar   The engine slows
And stops
We're here
We're finally here
I don't know how many days
Weeks
Months
It took
I lost track of time
Of how far we'd come
I felt different
As if I'd changed
Older
Wiser
More like a man
I should be happy
I should be smiling
Part of me was
But I was also sad
Sad for Houda
I had seen plenty of death in my home country
And it was always painful
To see it happen to other families

But when it happens to you
To your friend
It's more painful
Than you can imagine
I'd walk
And repeat the journey
Over and over
Ten times
A hundred times
If it meant
Houda could be here
The train doors open
To a huge crowd
On the platform
Standing behind barriers
Some holding big placards
Saying 'You are welcome here!'
Cheers
Clapping
And finally
That word

Crowd 3   *Willkommen!*
Willkommen!
Willkommen!

Jigsaw

A Play for Young People

Sumerah Srivastav

Lyrics by Ajay Srivastav

Author's Note

The idea for *Jigsaw* came about following a number of workshops with Year 10 students from Robert Clack School in Dagenham. Facilitated by director Julia Voce, the workshops aimed to uncover stories and characters for the piece by exploring the histories, connections and perceptions of the students in response to the theme of migration.

We worked on a number of exercises which included discussion, physical movement, role play and creative writing, as well as written responses to archive photos provided by the Migration Museum. The combined input of the students was gold dust and I was left with pages of material to go through including large cut-outs of two characters created by them to get me started!

It was clear to me that there were so many great ideas, situations and characters that it would be a shame not to try and include as many as I could. So, I constructed a play that would allow many stories to be told within a larger whole. I believe this form encapsulates the idea that there is no one story of migration and our attitude towards migrants says something about who we are and how we fit into this world, hence the title – *Jigsaw*.

My heartfelt thanks to Fin Kennedy, Emily Miller, Julia Voce, Miss H. Hamid, Sam Butler and all the students of Year 10.

Notes on Text

Jigsaw can be performed by any number and composition of actors.

Gender, where referenced in dialogue, can generally be switched – 'he' for 'she', 'mother' for 'father', etc. Some singular voices could be made plural – 'we' for 'I', etc.

A line that's just an ellipsis (. . .) is a moment where the speaker takes a pause.
A slash (/) is where the speaker is interrupted.
A new line (–) usually indicates a change of speaker.

Angels I

Large-cast piece.

Heaven. Three Angels: **Creation, Sustenance** *and* **Destruction**.

Sustenance *brings a chair onto an empty stage and sits facing the audience.*

Sustenance   So we all know it's not going to last forever, right? Nothing ever does. But while I've got you here I'm going to try my best to make this enjoyable and last as long as possible. That's my job – to sustain. As Sustenance I keep things going.

Creation *enters.*

Sustenance   It's not the most glamorous job, I'll admit. Take Creation. She's always so exciting. New things are constantly happening with her. New opportunities, adventure. Bright new stars, worlds, lifeforms. Ideas bubbling everywhere.

Creation *smiles. Silent.*

Sustenance   Trust me it's all happening between those ears.

Destruction *enters.*

Sustenance   Then there's Destruction. Never a dull moment with him. He's all about explosions, special effects, pure drama. I get the boring job. Churning out life day in, day out. Not that I'm complaining. After all today is different, special, 'cause you're here we've got guests. (*Motions to the audience.*) I'm not sure we've ever . . .? (*Looks enquiringly to* **Creation** *who shakes her head.*) See. It's never happened. So this is a first for all of us . . .

Destruction   Sustenance?

Sustenance (*to* **Destruction**)   One minute. (*Continues to audience.*) And you're all here for a story which works for us because where we're from, you know hanging out in the infinite, you come across one or two of those /

Destruction (*quietly to* **Sustenance**)   I need to talk to you.

Sustenance (*to* **Destruction** *through gritted teeth*)   Not now, can't you see I'm busy?

Destruction   I need to tell you something.

Sustenance   Later. We've got company.

Destruction (*to audience*)   Sorry. (*To* **Sustenance**.) I really think you should hear this. Matter of life or death.

Sustenance   It always is with you. Go on, then, quick.

Destruction   What, here?

Sustenance   Yes, here.

Destruction   I can't. It needs to be in private.

Sustenance   If it's something worth hearing then you can tell it here.

Destruction *considers the audience and smiles nervously at them.*

Destruction   Nah, you're alright.

Sustenance   You sure?

Destruction   We'll catch up later.

Sustenance   Can I carry on now?

Destruction   Yeah.

Sustenance   Where was I? Yeah, stories. How about this: you all took a journey to get here so let's talk about them – those journeys. The big ones, the little ones, the insignificant and the unforgettable. But where to start?

Suddenly a rush of full ensemble cast on stage.

Ensemble
– Over here!
– Yo!
– I've got one
– No let me do it

Sustenance *throws his hands up to stop the rabble.*

Sustenance   Stop! (*Selecting someone at random.*) You.

Ensemble
– He'll ruin it
– Why you gotta say that?
– This ain't about you
– Listen, fam, that's where you're wrong
– This is all about me
– And me
– And me
– Me too
– Hello?

Sustenance   Alright, alright! You can *all* tell it

Ensemble (*to audience*)   And guess what?
– What we've gotta say is about you too
– No one can escape their truth
– It's about all of us
– Right here
– Right now
– But before now
– Before we got here
– Before we came
– Conquered
– Created a home
– Together
– Then it falls apart
– Again
– And again
– And again
– But we put ourselves back together
– Each time
– Do we?
– We do
– We pretend we do
– We're good at pretending
– It's what we do
– Like a game
– Putting the pieces of ourselves back together
– We look good
– Don't we?
– A jigsaw, that's us
– With all the pieces
– In the right place

Sustenance   The thing is . . . Can you put a jigsaw back together when you've left a few of the pieces behind?

All look back to where they've 'come from'. Beat. Then scatter.

Sustenance   So let's do this piece by piece. Stories about being together, about fitting in, like this one . . .

£10

Small-cast piece. The story of one man's journey.

Sustenance   . . . about a man who crossed a border with just /

Ensemble
– Ten pound in his pocket
– Ten pound in his pocket and dirt in his shoes
– He came with dreams so big in his head he thought his mind would explode
– But nowhere did he have to go
– Arrived. He is still
– He looks down to the ground that his mucky shoes rest on
– He peers past them expecting to be standing on gold
– But the pavement is grey. No gold paves his way
– No women greet by falling at his feet
– This is not what he'd hoped . . .
– But it's good
– Good to be anonymous
– Good to be free
– Good for his family
– Those waiting at home for him to bring back plenty from this land unknown

– Ten pound in his pocket
– Ten pound to double, to treble, to exceed and succeed
– He gets to work
– No help is offered. No guiding hand
– The message in fact is to leave
– Go back
– No one wants you here
– Does he listen? Is he hurt? Will he turn away?
– When the doors slam and the heads shake no
– Does he listen? Is he hurt? Can he still stay?
– When the windows shatter and his ribs are broken
– Does he listen? Is he hurt? Why doesn't he go back?
– When the quiet and the cold settle into his bones
– Does he . . .? Is he . . .? Should he . . .?

– Ten pound in his pocket
– Ten pound in his pocket weighs heavy on him
– There's no corner he can cut

– No step he can skip
– He goes on and on
– And on and on
– Tired and weathered
– And battered and bruised
– Alone he goes on
– Not knowing if he'll ever find the plenty to send back home
– Time passes
– The cold is not so searing
– The language not so cutting
– His youth fades
– But his will power stays
– And a life is made
– For the journey he has taken there is no easy path
– But the footprints he leaves behind
– Guide the way
– For me, to be me
– Standing tall, resting . . .
– In my clean white shoes
– And the plenty he creates
– Is ten pound in *my* pocket

Sustenance   See that? Now that's a journey and a legacy, course not the one he intended but, still, not everyone manages both. For some people it's a miracle that they leave at all. I get it it's a big decision so I'm not surprised if your conscious mind was to doubt itself . . .

Escape

Medium-cast piece. The thoughts inside a conscious mind.

Ensemble
– Escape. Breathe free. Become a better me. I could be happy.
– Who do I think I am?
– What's so special about me?
– This should be enough
– How can I leave my family?
– When all I am is what they've given me
– Who's going to look after them?
– Not me.
– Escape. Breathe free. Become a better me. I could be happy.
– I know nothing about the law

– The land
– Or the language.
– Will I fail?
– Will I fit in?
– Will they accept me?
– What if I make the wrong decision? I'm never coming back
– Escape. Breathe free. Become a better me. I could be happy.
– I can't do this, I don't want to go
– I should give up now before I go
– Escape.
– Breathe free.
– Become a better me?

All   – Can I be happy?

Ensemble
– I don't know
– I could try.
– I may never be whole but . . .

All   – I will overcome.

Sustenance   That's what I'm talking about. Hope. Making a decision and having the courage to see it through. It's exciting. Course then there's those that don't think. Their heart makes the decision for them.

Forget Me Not I

Medium-cast piece.

Love roulette.

Ensemble
– He loves me
– He loves me not
– He loves me
– He loves me not
– He loves me.
– We'd never met before. Our families had lived opposite each other for generations. And yet my eyes and his smile had never found each other.
– It was cold that summer. Just my luck really. To go 'back home' with my mum the one time the tropical sun decided to do a runner. I'm miserable. My mum suggests hanging out in the sugar cane fields, it's

what she used to do when she was younger. I try it. I don't get what the attraction is. Until I see him.

– Let me tell you about love. Love is maths. One plus one equals two, right? Wrong.
– One plus one actually equals eighteen thousand and six hundred pounds.
– That is the true cost of love – per year.

– At first communication is . . . difficult. He explains he's a nurse working in France. I tell him I'm a student from London. And we laugh at how we've met as neighbours in a country neither of us actually live in. This exchange takes about an hour. My broken creole and his single-word English is laughable but we get by.
– I will tell you this though – it's amazing how much the right hand holding yours can say. You know what I mean?
– The monsoon weather turns out to be more perfectly romantic than all the rays of sunshine could ever be. I blink and two weeks have passed. Now I can't imagine going home and not seeing his smile everyday . . . I'm miserable all over again. But then the day before we leave his parents meet my mum. Promises are made and the smiles return for everyone.

– You'd think we'd have the right to choose . . . but as a British citizen who we love is actually a government thing. For people in power to decide.
– Marriage alone is not enough to keep couples together even if it was under the eyes of God.
– Forms have to be filled. Interviews conducted. Convincing to be done. Oh and also the price has to be paid . . .

– But my part-time wage doesn't make the grade.
– Long-distance love is . . . long. It has to be strong to travel over borders. Thank God for technology. Skype, Facebook, Messenger, text and phone calls – we've done the lot.
– Occasionally we've met up in person, face to face . . . He comes to me, me to him and it's amazing . . . even though each time it gets a little more difficult.
– I notice his smile is more strained and he can see what's going on behind my eyes without me even saying.
– I didn't realise how high the price tag was on love. After three years, the system is getting to me, to us.
– And we're beginning to hate on our love . . .

Sustenance   Sad isn't it? Not being allowed to be with someone you love.

Destruction   Heart-breaking. But for some, staying put isn't an option. And even though they don't want to leave – they must. Don't believe me? Try it for yourself. Let's meditate on this, shall we?

Lottery

Large-cast piece.

A family portrait.

– Close your eyes.

Destruction (*to audience*)   She's talking to you, guys. Go on. Close your eyes. That's it. Good.

– Now think of home. Where is it? Who lives with you? Whoever they are, those people, the ones that you care about most in the world, they're with you.
– Your mum, your dad. Brothers, sisters. Can you see them?
– What are you all doing? Are you smiling at each other and holding hands?
– Okay, so maybe you're arguing instead. Over what's on TV or who's turned off the WiFi. Whatever it is, it's normal and it feels like home to you. Where you belong.
– You banter
– And then whoever is in charge of dinner calls for you. It's your favourite meal. Happy days.
– And you munch on that food quick time.
– Someone cracks a joke and you laugh, spitting your food out all over the place and that just makes everyone laugh more
– At you
– But you don't mind. Your belly is full.
– What do you mean, 'What about dessert?'
– Okay, fine. Dessert . . . Now you're full. Dinner is officially over and you're in your bedroom.
– You get into your scuzzy lazy ripped-up home clothes. You know the ones. I know you know the ones. We've all got them.
– Your shoes are off and you feel the familiar soft carpet between your toes before slumping back onto your bed. Lying there you look up at the ceiling. Your ceiling. It's not a sight many have seen . . .
– Or have they?

– You're totally relaxed. You take a deep breath in. One long slow breath.

All cast take a deep breath in and out.

– Wait.
– You smell something.
– Smoke
– You get up to smell again
– Someone's gone and burnt toast
– You hope. But then you hear them
– The screams
– Screams from your family. Your mum, your dad. Brothers, sisters.
  They're calling you. You open the door.
– A heat like you've never felt before hits your face.
– Your home is ablaze
– Flames everywhere. The smoke blinds you and you cough your guts
  out. You can't breathe
– But you can hear.
– You follow a familiar voice. That voice turns into a hand that grabs you
  and pulls you out of your home.
– Strong. Rough. Desperate.
– You're outside.
– You're safe.
– Your family are with you. Can you see them?
– You hold hands, grateful.
– Happy to be alive and together.
– Your home however is destroyed. You call 999
– But the line is dead.
– You call the local police station, your cousin, your friend, your
  neighbour, your councillor even. Anyone who can help.
– No one answers.
– You scream out loud.
– A collective cry for help from everyone in your family to anyone on
  your street who will listen.
– But the lights are turned out one by one.
– You look at one another. You don't know what to say or do. You have
  nothing and no one but yourselves.
– You look down the end of the road and see a light.
– It's small but visible.
– Together you walk down the road. Hand in hand.
– Away from your home
– Towards the light
– Praying it won't go out.

Sustenance   Okay. No need to make everyone feel bad.

Destruction   But do they though, do they really get it?

Sustenance   Course they do. Life's a lottery. You deal with the hand you're given the best way you know how. They get it.

Destruction   Good. 'Cause people turning a blind eye is why some get away with this next story.

Forget Me Not II

Medium-cast piece.

Love roulette gone wrong.

Ensemble
– He loves me
– He loves me not
– He loves me
– He loves me not
– He loves me
– He loves me not.
– I was at the top of my class, that's why, he says, he chose me
– 'You're wasted here'
– He says
– 'There are better opportunities for someone bright like you. If you're
    brave enough I can arrange it'
– But I haven't finished my studies I say
– 'Why be a nurse here when you could be a doctor over there? I need
    your answer by tomorrow.'
– I decide. I want to make my parents proud.
– To help them out of struggle
– There are so many things I don't know.
– I don't know where I am
– I don't know when I'll eat
– I don't know if the sun has come out today
– Or when they speak what they say

– He is charming, intelligent, organised and quick. I've never been on a
    plane before.
– He says 'Just do as I say and everything will be okay'.
– And my parents? I ask.

– 'Your parents will be proud when you tell them how far you've come
   on your own'.
– When? I ask.
– 'Be patient, have faith, you are meant for greatness'.
– And that is the truth I believe. Until he forces me into a room. A room I
   won't leave for the next eleven months.

– These things I convince myself to forget.
– The dark, the cold, the feeling of growing old.
– The pain, too much for one heart to contain.
– The blood from being beaten,
– Forced time and again into every meeting.
– I don't know what they pay
– I just do what they ask and pray.

– I'm home again.
– Like a dream.
– The familiar faces I've longed to see now in front of me
– I say nothing. I can't speak. My shame stops me from even raising my
   gaze.
– Then I hear their voices.
– 'We all walk amongst our own demons'
– 'But you, my child, have fought the worst of them and survived'
– I cry.
– For their pride.
– For forgiveness.
– For home.

Destruction   She's lucky, she went back to a family who loved her
who'd shelter her. But there are hundreds, thousands of others who don't
. . . Argh I'm getting vexed

Sustenance (*worried*)   Alright, alright, calm down.

Sustenance *moves* **Destruction** *away from the audience to where*
Creation *is.*

Angels II

Small named cast piece.

Heaven.

Sustenance   It's okay.

Destruction   Yeah but it ain't. They never listen.

Sustenance   Free will is a killer.

Creation *nods sagely.*

Destruction   We can't just sit here and do nothing.

Sustenance   We're helping . . . from afar. It's what we do.

Destruction   It's not enough.

Sustenance   The boss says we do signs so we do signs.

Destruction   Forget signs, they've got it all written down anyway. 'The stranger who stays with you in your land shall be as a native from among you and you should love him as yourself.' Moses, man, Moses. But do they listen?

Sustenance (*shakes head sadly/ironically*)   'Mankind we have created you from male and female and made you peoples and tribes so that you may know one another.' Muhammad.

Creation   'Glory to God in the highest and on Earth peace and good will toward men'.

Sustenance *and* **Destruction** *look at* **Creation** *in amazement for having said something.*

Destruction (*to* **Sustenance**)   She speaks?

Sustenance   Sometimes. (*To* **Creation**.) We did Christianity already, Creation.

Creation (*shakes his head*)   Luke, Judaism.

Sustenance/Destruction (*realising*)   Oh yeah.

Destruction   The point is how many different ways can we say, 'The whole world is one family'? That's been written since the days of Sanskrit.

Sustenance   I know . . . This one is a relative, that one's a stranger. They're not clever. I'll give you that.

Destruction   I'm not even asking for clever. I just want them to open their eyes. I'm telling you, even when you've arrived doesn't mean it's over, you gotta deal with the natives – getting either dissed or dismissed. Check it out.

Lodger I

Small-cast piece.

A sitting room. A teenager playing a video game is surprised when a non-white girl with her head covered enters. She makes a small nod of acknowledgement to him and then exits upstairs.

– Mum! Mum! Mum!
– What's all the yelling for? Are you alright?
– Someone just swanned in here, a girl I think, didn't you see her? She went upstairs.
– A girl?
– Yes.
– Just now?
– Yes just now!
– Is that it? I thought it was something serious with all that screaming. It's not good for my stress levels.
– Mum? Mum! MUM!!
– Don't you take that tone with me. That was just Nadia, my lodger.
– You've got a lodger?
– Yes. Charming girl, very well mannered.
– Living here?
– Yes. She's been . . . staying in your room.
– You rented out my room?!
– Remember we talked about this. A halfway house for people who need it. And anyway you weren't here.
– I was on a gap year! Travelling. Meaning I was gonna come back.
– Alright. Well I didn't know that did I? She'll be leaving tomorrow.
– When were you gonna tell me about her?
– Well, you haven't been very talkative since you got back this morning so . . .
– How long have you had her?
– She's not a cat.
– She smells of curry.
– She's lovely. And a great help to me so you be nice to her. She's had a tough time of it so I expect you to do the charitable thing and at least be polite to her face.
– There's charity and then there's charity, Mum. You shouldn't just let a complete stranger into our home. It could be dangerous.
– She was in need. Terrible story.
– So give her some money and send her somewhere else.
– Should I have done that with you?

– It's not the same thing.

– You were brought up better than this.

– She could be anyone, some crazed fundamentalist nutter. They train
      women too you know, don't you watch the news?

– I think she's great. She pays her way and is absolutely no bother. Apart
      from being a little sensitive about a few things . . .

– What things?

– Pork, alcohol, animals. That sort of thing.

– See!

– Honestly she's as quiet as a mouse.

– That's not always a good thing. You know it's always the quiet ones.

– What do you mean?

– One word. Isis.

– Oh for Heaven's sake!

– I'm serious, Mum.

– So am I, young man.

– Okay, fine . . . but people like her should be paying rent like everyone
      else. No special treatment.

Destruction   'No special treatment', that's a nice idea, makes sense.
Except not everyone is treated equally in reality. Like the rental market,
not exactly welcoming to some . . . Take these two landladies. The
Knagg sisters.

We Don't Have a Problem

Medium-cast piece.

*A rental flat. Its owners, the Knagg sisters, have joined their lettings
agent while hosting an open house to prospective tenants who are milling
around the flat.*

*The text in italics can be sung. There is a choral part for the group of
neighbours in the song and the tenants are featured through action.*

– Don't forget to show them the gas and electric certificates.

– And please watch their feet we really don't want heel marks on our
      new floor.

– Yes, Miss Knagg

– Oh and did I mention we repainted the bedroom?

– Rose meadow, much better don't you think?

– It really is lovely, Miss Knagg. Just as lovely as it was yesterday.

– Well as long as you have everything you need.

– I do. Was there anything else?

– (*sotto*) You will be careful won't you? In vetting the prospectives?

– Of course. We always request references from our tenants.

– Right . . .

– Did you want to stay for the open house, Miss Knagg and Miss
    Knagg?

– Oh no no, of course not . . .

– It's just . . .

– You must understand that the Knagg family have lived in this area for
    generations.

– We've a lot of history here and I wouldn't want to upset my neighbours
    with, erm, with . . .

– A certain sort.

– Sort?

– Well . . .

We don't have a problem,
For us it's all good
But they always tend to talk
Round our neighbourhood.

Once a couple had a bother
You know, bit of a shout
And before you knew it
the neighbours had them out.

We don't have a problem
Next door may cause a fuss
They like a certain kind of person
You know, a bit like us?
The neighbours over here
Like hobnobs with their tea
I'm not sure they'd deal readily
With . . . diversity?

(*Neighbours' choral section.*)

They've had curry with an Indian
They donate to Bangladesh
Their best friend's sister's auntie
Had a coloured at her creche.
But to be fair you must agree
They're not sure who to trust
Perhaps there is a fear that
There'll be more of them than us?

During this last section the agent introduces **Miss Knagg** *to prospective tenants whom she dismisses out of hand until there are no tenants left.*

> *We don't have a problem*
> *I'm not one of 'those'*
> *But some say British culture*
> *Is now suffering some blows*
> *They say they're coming for our benefits*
> *And perhaps your job, my dear,*
> *So let's do what's best for all of us*
> *They think it's best for all of us*
> *Don't you agree it's best for all of us*
> *That they don't come here!*

– All the tenants have left.
– Oh dear.
– Will there be more?
– I hope so, Miss Knagg.

Angels III

Heaven.

Named cast.

Destruction   So there it is.

Sustenance   There what is?

Destruction   It. The whole thing. People treating each other like...
It's gonna just keep happening no matter what we do so we may as well admit defeat.

Sustenance   And do what?

Destruction   I've got a plan.

Sustenance   A plan?

Destruction   It's what I was trying to tell you before.

Sustenance   The thing you wanted to say in private?

Destruction *nods.*

Sustenance   What is it?

Destruction *is apprehensive with one eye on the audience.*

Sustenance   Don't worry we're among friends now.

Destruction   I've been thinking and I believe it's for the best.

I'm going down to sort them out.

This is big news. **Sustenance** *looks to* **Creation** *who hangs her head low.*

Creation   What?!

Sustenance   Are you out of your mind?! You can't. Why would you do that?

Destruction   They need it.

Sustenance   They always need it but that doesn't mean we do *that* to them.

Destruction   Look at them down there. It's mayhem. They're turning their backs on each other. It's just plain rude . . .

Sustenance   Trust me I'm all about helping. Part of the job description. Just do it from up here is all I'm saying. No need to get your wings dirty.

Destruction   Signs, words, messages even conscience – none of it makes a difference. I *have* to go.

Sustenance   Give them time.

Destruction   How much time?

Sustenance (*looks at the audience, working it out*)   A couple of millennia?

Destruction (*shakes his head*)   I can't. The boss has had enough.

Sustenance   Are you saying what I think you're saying?

Destruction   It's over for them.

Destruction *goes to exit.*

Sustenance   Destruction, no!

Creation *stands in front of* **Destruction** *blocking his path.* **Destruction** *stops.*

Sustenance   Please wait.

Destruction   Why do you even care?

Sustenance   You know why.

Destruction   But aren't you tired, Sustenance? Of maintaining their existence? And you, Creation, admit it; you made a mistake, a big one. It's not like we haven't got loads elsewhere to be getting on with. They're a tiny planet in a corner galaxy. I bet tomorrow you won't even notice they're gone and we'll be better for it.

Sustenance   Please? They're not all bad. Listen . . .

Postcards Back Home

Large-cast piece.

A row of speakers say one-liners that they write down intended for their respective family left behind.

(*Option to add more positive single-line experiences.*)

– It's sunnier than I thought.
– Seriously, like random people just come up to me and touch my hair.
– I'd give anything for some rambutan right now.
– You get used to it, you just get by.
– I want to stay now, this is home.
– He's foreign but nice.
– I can send you some money now, it's not much but it's mine.
– She didn't have to help me, but she did.
– Seven. I have seven employees, people relying on me.

Once said, the speakers fold their thoughts into paper planes and fly them into the sky. They land at **Destruction**'s *feet.*

Sustenance   See? They find a way to make it work.

Destruction   Making it work isn't enough anymore, they need to find a way to fit together.

Sustenance   Okay, so what about this – it hasn't happened yet but it will (*looks at watch*) in about four hours and twelve minutes this is gonna happen . . .

Destruction   What's that?

Sustenance   Remember the teenager and the lodger, they erm . . . chat.

Lodger II

Large-cast piece.

The rap is delivered as a battle rap with 'clapped' beats and opposing sides. Suggested girls versus boys.

Boy
(Damn) I just come home
I don't need this crap
Some random foreigner
Laying out a trap
I'm not being funny
But this is my house.
My gaff, my rules
And you have got to get out.
Who knows what you're keeping
Tucked under the beds
Who knows what you're plotting
I better call the Feds
I know your lot, making trouble
Everywhere you go
Taking all our benefits
I read the news y'know
Yeah I see the truth
I got the eyes of an eagle
I don't mean to be funny
But are you even legal?

Girl
Oh, okay.
The prodigal son returned
Trotted round the globe
But you still never learned
The idea of tolerance,
Peace and respect
So many cultures and people
In the world to accept?
Nah, I bet you just followed
In your forefathers' steps
Y'know the ones who built an empire
Without an inch of regret
For the blood that they spilled,
For the things that they stole

For the countries they destroyed,
Divided and owned
Nah you don't give a shit,
You don't wanna know the truth
That they created this monster
That's now on the loose
Cos you have the luxury,
The luxury to blame
A life of entitlement
So for you it's a game.
So play on with your game
And your lame little rants
Play on with your beer
And your skinny jean pants
Play on with your brain
The size of an ant
You don't know who I am,
You just label me
Put me in a box
Take away my right to be.

Boys' Posse
Nah, bruv, she's just full of lies
We can see the violence and evil in her eyes
We bet she's here with a plan to terrorise
Go on . . . ask her where her loyalties lie.

Girls' Posse
Did he just say that?
Did he really go there?
Some people in this world
Are beyond a prayer.

Boys' Posse
Ahh . . . look at her
Playing the victim
They can't be trusted
Better restrict and evict them.

Girls' Posse
Stand your ground
This is our home now
There ain't no need
To scrape and bow.

All Boys
You don't belong
Get out now.

All Girls
No, you are wrong
This is our home now.

All Boys
You don't belong
Get out now.

All Girls
No, you are wrong
This is our home now.

Destruction   This is not helping your cause.

Sustenance   Stay with it.

Girl
No this ain't me
This ain't what I'm about
I got nothing against you
With your fear and doubt.
If you really wanna know
What hits me like a shot
I see what I don't have
In everything that you got.
I ain't talking 'bout your room
Or your money or your keys
I'm talking 'bout your freedom and your liberty.
The freedom to not be judged by the clothes I wear
The freedom to not be watched with suspicious stares
I just got love in my heart it's all I wanna give
Why can't I just be me? Live and let live.

Boy
(What?!) Girl, are you kidding me?
You think you got problems, take a look at me
I ain't exactly all I'm cracked up to be
I got all my life lessons watching daytime TV
I get knocked down too
No one's got my back
My life ain't so sorted

I ain't got no hack
Look I didn't mean to judge you
You just made me feel
A little insecure
Like I'm no big deal
It ain't me neither
I was just chattin' shit
Felt a bit threatened
Okay, look, let's call it quits . . .

Both
We got the same troubles
And you're not to blame
So let's just agree
Deep down we're all the same.

All
We got the same troubles
And you're not to blame
So let's just agree
Deep down we're all the same
We got the same troubles
And you're not to blame
So let's just agree
Deep down we're all the same.

Angels IV

Large-cast piece.

Sustenance   Good, huh? Admit it. I saw your head bouncing!

Destruction   It doesn't change anything.

Sustenance   But it could. They can do this, Destruction. On the rare
occasions that they recognise themselves in each other they are . . . good.
Good humans. Worth keeping.

Destruction   What are you saying?

Sustenance   Let them learn. If enough of them find a way to fit together
then they'll have peace and we wouldn't have failed.

Destruction   Says you, but I don't see them saying the same thing.
Turn your back and they'll be at each other again. They can't be trusted.

Creation *whistles or motions to the ensemble to prompt them into speaking to back up* **Sustenance**.

Ensemble
– We can!
– Mostly.
– We are different but
– We've all made journeys
– Over land
– In our minds
– Between our hearts
– But here
– We all are
– Does that make us the same?
– No
– The path we've travelled is our own
– Our edges are different from what they were before
– So the jigsaw we used to fit in
– Don't fit no more.
– But we can find our place
– In a new jigsaw
– Allow us to learn, to settle in and fit
– Yeh it'll be hard
– Yeh it'll take time
– But let's face it.
– None of us wants to be left behind
– On the outside
– Of the jigsaw.

Sustenance   So, Destruction? Are you going to give them that chance? Are you gonna hang back?

Destruction (*pause as he looks around him, considering*)   What do you expect me to tell the boss?

Sustenance   You'll think of something.

Destruction   Alright, fine. I'll leave them be. (*As a warning.*) For now.

Sustenance *smiles, satisfied.* **Creation** *high-fives some of the ensemble while the rest rush at* **Destruction** *happy to have saved humanity.*

All cast end in a tableau linking themselves together. A completed jigsaw.

Exercises

A selection of the exercises from the first workshop day is included below.

The first section includes exercises used at the start of the session to explore the theme of migration, defining certain terms and discussing students' personal experiences of, and/or perceptions of, migration. This is followed by a section of drama games and more involved exercises to generate characters and stories.

It is not necessary to use every single exercise below – this was just the pool from which our writer–director teams mixed and matched, and sometimes added their own, so each first workshop day was different in each school.

We include these exercises here in a similar spirit, so that teachers can dip in and explore this theme and create their own plays in their own ways. None of these exercises alone will generate a fully formed play, but they will generate numerous interesting fragments which a writer can be tasked with stitching together into a script between sessions.

Teachers do not have to complete these exercises across a whole day as we did; they are of course free to develop their own plays across several timetabled periods or after school. In this case, we would recommend the teacher either taking the lead in the role of playwright and bringing newly written material into each session (inspired by the previous week's session) to build the play up bit by bit, or they could appoint a small writing team from among the students to take this task on.

At the end of this section is some advice on techniques to write large-cast ensemble plays to accommodate larger groups. It is also possible, of course, to use the same process to create several smaller plays, perhaps linked, for smaller casts, then to perform them one after the other. It really is up to you.

Section 1: Exercises to unpack the theme of migration

Exercise: *What's in a name?*

Set-up: Participants sit in a circle on chairs or the floor. This is usually the first activity of the workshop.

Teacher instructions: Invite everybody in the circle, one by one, to say their name. It can be their first name, their middle name or their surname.

Then go round again and ask each student to share with the group one thing about their name. It could be one of the following:

- What your name means.
- Which language or culture is associated with your name.
- Do you like your name?
- Who gave you your name?
- If you were a boy/girl what would you have been called instead?
- What would you prefer to be called if you weren't given your name?

Notes: Pupils generally respond very positively to this activity, especially if it is used as the first activity of the workshop. Most people like sharing something about themselves, but of course people can be given the option to 'pass'. The teacher must be ready to positively respond to each name and to keep this activity flowing.

We find that this activity inevitably brings up some migration references, and then these can be explored further in the subsequent activities

Exercise: *Line-out*

Set-up: This activity requires a fairly large space, so if in a classroom, desks will need to be moved to the side. Pupils are invited to stand either in one line shoulder to shoulder, or in a circle facing inwards.

Teacher instructions: Introduce the activity by saying that this is a chance to explore connections to migration in the group. Explain that you are going to offer statements one by one and that if this statement refers to a pupil's experience, their family experience or their opinion, that they are invited to take a small step forward from the line or from the circle.

You might give a practice statement just to make sure everybody understands the activity, such as: 'take a small step forwards if you are a pupil at X School'.

Then the teacher makes one statement after another. Below are some suggestions:

- If you/your parents/grandparents were born abroad.
- If you speak a different language at home.
- If you have friends from a different culture/religion.
- If you have lived in a different country for more than three months of your life.
- If you eat food that has migrated from different cultures.
- If you have moved from one city to another in the UK.

- If you support a football team with at least five immigrant players.
- If you listen to music that has migrated, or by musicians that have migrated.
- If you know someone who has been forced to leave their country: an asylum seeker or a refugee.
- If you want to emigrate: live and work abroad in the future.

Notes: After this, the facilitator can ask the pupils some discussion questions, such as:

- Why did we do this activity?
- Who took a step at some point?
- What did we learn from this activity?
- Were there any statements you didn't understand?
- What statements would you add if you were a facilitator?'

Exercise: *Your world map*

Set-up: This activity requires a fairly large space, so if in a classroom, desks will need to be moved to the side. Encourage pupils to come and stand with you in one line along the long edge of the space. Without worrying too much about precise geography, ask pupils to look at the empty space in front of them and picture the world map. If you have a printed world map handy then perhaps have it pinned to the wall and make reference to it. The instruction is for pupils to move around their world map based on a series of stimulus questions you provide one by one. Some of these could be:

- Go and stand where you were born.
- Go and stand where one of your parents/grandparents was born.
- Go and stand in a country you've always wanted to visit.
- Go and stand in a country where a friend of yours is from or has their family roots.
- Go and stand in a country where you've been on holiday and might consider living.
- Go and stand in a country where there is conflict that is leading to refugee movements.
- Go and stand in a country many people want to move to for its strong economy.

Notes: At any point you can pause the activity and select pupils to explain which country they are standing in and why they are there.

After moving around the map a few times, initiate a discussion with the pupils where you can explore a few questions:

- What did you like about that activity?
- What did you find challenging about that activity?
- Did you discover anything new about your fellow students from doing the activity?
- What other statements would you have added in?

Exercise: *Defining terms*

Set-up: This exercise can be done in a normal classroom with desks, or in a drama studio on the floor. You will need to type up and print several copies of the table below. Add a right-hand column left blank for students to fill in their answers in small groups. You could distribute different terms to each student then transcribe them all to the board for everyone to see. Alternatively, you could give out blank paper and read out the terms like a pub quiz, asking students to define them. The most correct answers wins a prize.

Teacher instructions: People often have misconceptions around certain terms related to migration. Ask your students to define the following, then compare with the definitions below and discuss any differences.

Keyword	Definition
Migration	People moving from one place to another
Immigration	The act of someone coming to live in a different country
Emigration	The act of someone leaving to go and live in a different country
Migrant	Someone who moves from one place to another in order to live in another country for more than a year. (The International Organization for Migration estimates that 232 million people a year become international migrants and another 740 million move within their own countries.)
Refugee	A person who has fled their country due to well-founded fear of persecution for political, religious or ethnic reasons, or because of war.
Asylum Seeker	Someone who has left their own country, often for political reasons or because of war, and who has travelled to another country hoping that the government will protect them and allow them to live there.

Economic Migrant	Someone who leaves their country and moves to another in search of better economic opportunities.
Discrimination	Treating a person or particular group differently from how you treat others (in a negative way) because of their skin colour, gender, age, sexuality, etc.
Prejudice	An unfair and unreasonable opinion or feeling, especially when formed without enough thought or knowledge. Literally 'pre-judging' someone before you really know them.
Identity	Who a person is, or the qualities of a person or group that distinguishes them from others.
Diversity	A range of people with different skin colours, languages, beliefs, customs, etc.
Diaspora	A scattered population with a common origin in a smaller geographic area. Diaspora can also refer to the movement of the population from its original homeland.
Integration	The process of joining and becoming part of a new society or culture.

Exercise: *100 images*

Set-up: Photos have an ability to tell stories. This exercise uses a gallery of 100 images from the Migration Museum archive. If you have access to a colour printer a selection of these should be printed in advance (if you have a laminator they can be used again repeatedly or displayed on the classroom wall afterwards). Alternatively, give students the following link and ask them to choose a photo by browsing them on a computer screen in small groups: https://www.migrationmuseum.org/100imagesgallery.

You will also need several packs of post-it notes and pens.

Teacher instructions: Explain that images can be a great stimulus for improvisation and devising. Put students into small groups and ask them to choose a few photos. Writing their ideas on post-it notes, get them to consider various provocations:

- Who are the people in this photo and what is happening to them?
- What happened directly before/after this photo was taken?
- What would you ask if you met the person in the photo?

- Do you have any personal connection with the photo?
- What is the photographer trying to say to you through this photo?

Notes: Ask students to show their photos to the rest of the group and read out some of their ideas about what is happening. If there is time, ask them to stage the photo as a still image, then animate it, showing what happens next. This could form the basis for scenes within your play.

Some further exercises building on the 100 images:

- **Free-writing:** Choose a character from the image and write non-stop for three minutes on the thoughts of your chosen character.
- **Building physicality:** Find a space in the room and adopt the sleeping position of your character. Then get up and move as your character would as they go about their day. Questions can be asked to stimulate imagination: where they're going, what they're wearing or a problem they are facing.
- **Hot seating:** Students introduce themselves in character, and answer questions from the audience about their life, background and current situation.

Section 2: Drama games

Most drama teachers know hundreds of these. They're mostly for fun and work well as ice breakers when new groups don't know each other. Here are a few of our favourites which will get everyone ready for the improvisation exercises below.

Stop, Go, Jump, Clap

Ask the group to walk around the space. When you say *Stop* they freeze, *Go* means start walking again. Try this a few times. Then add in *Jump* and *Clap* as they are walking. Try this a few times. Then reverse everything: *Stop* means *Go*, *Go* means *Stop*, *Jump* means *Clap* and *Clap* means *Jump*. Build this up into combinations such as 'Jump, Clap, Jump, Go' and see if they can keep up.

Pass the pencil

One volunteer 'detective' is sent out while a pencil is given to one group member with others in a tight circle. They must pass the pencil around the circle without the detective guessing where it is.

Sharks

Put single pages of newspaper on the floor as islands, and explain that there is shark-infested water all around. The group are pearl fishers, out hunting in only swimwear. Sharks appear when the tutor shouts 'SHARKS!' and everyone has to take refuge on an island, with the last to do so getting eaten and having to sit out. Take away an island or two each time so there is less and less land to hide on. Other words beginning with 'sh' can be used to make sure they're paying attention (only 'sharks' should cause them to seek refuge). Repeat until only one fisherman is left – the winner.

Name the room

Students walk around the space and are first asked to point at things and name them: chair, table, wall, light, etc. Next, they point at things saying the name of the previous thing they were pointing at, stimulating memory. Finally, they point at things naming them anything but what they are: elephant, teapot, submarine, etc. This stimulates imagination and acceptance of spontaneous thought, vital skills in improvisation.

Tell us about . . .

Individuals are invited to '*tell us about*' a given subject such as their first home, an interesting journey they have made, their favourite country, a favourite family member, their ambition in life, somewhere they would like to visit. You can prep these in advance or ask the group to come up with some on slips of paper which are selected at random. Give each student thirty seconds to 'tell us about' the chosen stimulus, without pausing.

Section 3: Improvisation exercises

Exercise: *Lines of dialogue*

Set-up: Drama studio or large classroom with chairs cleared away. Each student is given five slips of paper and they need to write a line of dialogue related to migration on each one (you could recycle some of the thoughts on the post-it notes from the '100 Images' exercise above). The slips are collected and put together in a pile.

Teacher instructions: Get the group to choose a location linked to migration (e.g. airport, border checkpoint, passport office). Two actors sit on chairs in the 'room', the audience gives the actors an issue unrelated to the location for them to discuss (e.g. her missing hamster). A pile of dialogue lines is placed in front of them, on the floor. The rest of the group watches. The action starts and every so often the actors pick a slip of paper and build it into the conversation . . . the more bizarre the lines, the more interesting the drama gets.

Exercise: *Six-word plays*

Set-up: Drama studio or classroom with acting space cleared.

Teacher instructions: Tell the group it is possible to tell a story in six words. Rules of the game are:

- Two characters only, A and B
- Each says one word per line in turn, for six lines.

In advance, write and print off some six-word plays, in the following format. Try to inflect them with our theme of migration, for example:

Play 1		Play 2		Play 3	
A	Papers?	A	Swim.	A	Welcome.
B	Burned.	B	Can't.	B	Thanks.
A	Valuables?	A	Sinking.	A	Happy?
B	Lost.	B	Scared.	B	Sad.
A	Liar.	A	Try.	A	Rest.
B	Please.	B	Alright.	B	Sorry.

You can use these, or write your own.

Get two actors to read one out while the others watch. Then ask them:

- Who are these people?
- What is their relationship?
- Where are they?
- What is this about?
- What's just happened?
- What happens next?

Notes: After explaining the exercise, ask students to write their own six-word play on the theme of migration in pairs. Perform them back and ask the audience to interpret them.

After running the exercise a few times, you can use the scenarios which emerge as the basis for longer improvisations, giving the actors more words and allowing them to show what happens next.

Exercise: *Creating obstacles and conflict*

Set-up: Drama studio or cleared classroom. Whiteboard needed.

Teacher instructions: As a class, make a list of obstacles relating to migration, which might cause some kind of conflict for the migrant. Explain that obstacles and conflict are an important part of drama, because watching characters struggle to get what they want is how they learn and change. The best obstacles are often another character. Write their examples on the whiteboard. The list might include:

- Assembling what they need for a long journey.
- Applying for a visa.
- Booking a boat ticket.
- Saying goodbye to someone they love.
- Finding suitable food.
- Running out of money.
- Preparing for an interview at the border.
- Looking for work.
- Finding somewhere to stay.
- Meeting the locals.
- Communicating with home.

In threes or fours, choose one obstacle and rehearse a short improvisation in which A and B are migrants engaged in this activity. C and/or D stands in their way and could either help them or block them depending on how the scene goes. The dialogue is about A and B trying to persuade C and/or D to give them what they want.

Give the group five minutes' rehearsal time, then watch a few.

After each scene, ask the audience:

- What clues are in the scene about what the nature of the relationship is between the migrant characters?
- What tactics do they use to try to get what they want?
- How are they changed by the experience of dealing with this obstacle?
- What might they try next?

The final question can often lead to a second scene . . .

Other ideas

- Migration and the media: Source some newspaper headlines (or full articles if you have time) from now and in the past on the theme of migration. Get students to interrogate the real story behind the way it has been reported.

- Character journey: Have opposite walls of the room representing 'old home' and 'new home'. Ask pupils to walk slowly between old and new. Stop them at times to ask them how they feel at different points on the journey.

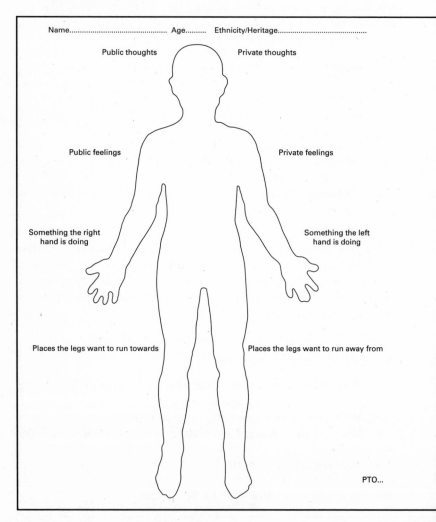

Name.. Age.......... Ethnicity/Heritage..

Public thoughts   Private thoughts

Public feelings   Private feelings

Something the right hand is doing   Something the left hand is doing

Places the legs want to run towards   Places the legs want to run away from

PTO...

- Phone home: In character, ask students to write or perform a phone call to relatives in the country they have left. What do they say to them about the journey they have been on? What news is there from home?

- This body outline handout is quite useful for empathetic character building. Once these sheets are complete get them to introduce their character to the group, then look for connections between them. They don't all have to be migrant characters; some could be friends they meet in their new school, for example.

Now answer these questions, as the character:

I love ....

....

I hate ....

....

I wish ....

....

I dream ....

....

Now, in groups:

Introduce your characters to one another. How do they know each other?

....

....

Which other characters do they like, and why?

....

Which characters don't they like, and why?

....

Tell us about a storyline which would involve your character:

....

....

....

General advice

- Use the breaks between sessions to assess what has emerged and build up the next exercise or session to develop the most promising ideas more fully. Those tasked with writing can write some script, however short, inspired by the previous session.
- Work out ways to include white British pupils, who may feel they have no migration connections. Examples might include migration to the UK from Ireland, or the UK's different regional identities.
- For pupils with English as an additional language, visual exercises and keywords can work well, such as 100 images.
- Allow time at the end of each session to discuss the material which has emerged. These reflections are often where the best ideas are sparked.
- Ensure you are aware of any important background information on members of the group, to avoid any upset or sensitivities about personal experiences.
- Do expect there to be prejudice and misunderstanding around this theme. Use the first section of exercises unpacking migration as a way to iron some of these out and create a safe atmosphere for all. Team games at the start also help.
- Don't be afraid to correct students about inaccuracies or misconceptions. It might be worth reading up on migration facts (and myths) in advance. The website Full Fact has a good immigration section: www.fullfact.org/immigration

Writing for large casts: some tips and techniques

The plays in this volume use a variety of techniques for accommodating large casts of young people. Here are some notes on these techniques, which can be used to create your own plays from scratch, or to write coursework essays about the plays in the volume and the techniques the writer has used and how this works in performance.

Individual named parts

All the plays in this volume use this to some extent, sometimes using a core of named parts supported by an ensemble of narrators. This technique prioritises larger parts for more confident performers to carry the play, with others in supporting roles. Drawbacks are that it can be difficult for each individual character to have a full story with a beginning, middle and end when the overall running time is quite short. Usually supporting characters and their journeys are arranged in relation to a main character and either assist or block that character in getting what they want.

Chorus/ensemble of narrators

Potato Moon by Satinder Chohan uses this technique. The chorus of Parakeets at the start can be played by two or more students, as can the Allotment Gang and The Trees, with really no upper limit on the amount of students these chorus roles can accommodate. Each new line is simply a new speaker. This technique allows for flexible cast sizes and if everyone learns everything then students can cover for each other in performance if one of them forgets their lines. This technique lends itself to a dynamic physical theatre acting style to bring scenes to life while speaking; it works less well if the lines are simply recited while standing still. The direct address technique also sets the scene very quickly, dispensing with the need for detailed set changes and allowing the play to move quite quickly though time and space. The ensemble can sometimes voice a character's unspoken thoughts, or give them lines they wish they'd said but didn't.

The main parts are played by more than one actor

In *Willkommen* by Asif Khan, the part of Ammar could be played by multiple actors, almost as if they are conflicting voices inside him, or different parts of his personality. A similar technique could be to have Ammar played by one actor at a time but changing over the course of the play, to suggest time passing and the character growing older or being changed by his experiences.

Crowd scenes

Nothing to Declare by Sharmila Chauhan uses this technique. Like ensemble lines, lines for crowds can just be distributed among the cast. Lines can also be improvised by giving the crowd a mood (elated, hostile, etc.) and allowing your cast to riff on that theme. Or you could put competing factions of a crowd into the same scene, to split into two as their disagreement emerges. Scenes in places where people gather, such as the border fence in *Willkommen*, can work in the same way, with large numbers of students miming activities to bring the location to life while the main characters walk through it delivering their lines.

The road trip

Having established your main character/s have them go on a long journey where they pass through lots of different locations and meet lots of different people in individual, chronological scenes. *Willkommen* does this.

Dream sequences

These can often involve stylised movement or characters representing memories, ghosts, demons, disembodied voices. etc., all of which create opportunities for several actors. In *Jigsaw* by Sumerah Srivastav, Angels look down on Earth and comment on the goings-on below. In *Willkommen,* Ammar has nightmares which could be brought to life by several different actors.

Inanimate objects come to life

Characters don't just have to be people. *In Nothing to Declare*, a series of significant objects are brought to life and given a voice and opinions about the people around them.

Physical theatre

Some of the best young people's plays involve large casts 'becoming' the location using physical representations. This works particularly well with natural locations like the allotment in *Potato Moon*. Combined with simple vocal sounds (birds squawking, etc.) the effect can be immediate and quite atmospheric. It also allows for such locations to suggest enchantment, e.g. moving trees. The same techniques can be applied to large vehicles or moving locations such as the boat journey in *Willkommen*.

Cast speak in unison

This can only really be used momentarily but it can be useful to suggest an intimidating presence like a god, monster or other authority figure. The Angels in *Jigsaw* or the Immigration Officers in *Nothing to Declare* could be played like this.